A

UNDER
ECKHART TOLLE

The Power of Living in the Now

2 Workbooks in 1: Living in The Now &
Stop Negative Thinking in Easy Steps

LESSONS & EXERCISES FOR BEGINNERS

THE SECRET OF NOW SERIES
GRAPEVINE BOOKS
2018

A. J.   P A R R

ALL RIGHTS RESERVED

AUTHOR: A. J. Parr.
Author Amazon Page: http://amazon.com/author/ajparr

COVER PHOTO TOLLE: Kyle Hoobin (Creative Commons) See in Wikipedia.

PHOTO DALAI LAMA/TOLLE: Kris Krug (Creative Commons) See in Wikimedia Commons.

PUBLISHED BY: Grapevine Books (Ediciones De La Parra) edicionesdelaparra@gmail.com

ISBN-13: 978-1983978500

ISBN-10: 1983978507

THE SECRET OF NOW SERIES

VOLUME 1

Living in "The Now" in Easy Steps

https://www.amazon.com/dp/B00J57TQZO

VOLUME 2

Buddhist Meditation For Beginners

https://www.amazon.com/dp/B00JE54A8K

VOLUME 3

Spiritual Hindu Tales to Calm Your Mind

https://www.amazon.com/dp/B00JJZLCBI

VOLUME 4

Christian Meditation in Easy Steps

https://www.amazon.com/dp/B00KLHUG7Y

VOLUME 5

Meditation in 7 Easy Steps

https://www.amazon.com/dp/B01L9DRF9U

VOLUME 6

Stop Negative Thinking in 7 Easy Steps

https://www.amazon.com/dp/B00MVLI6JI

VOLUME 7

Understanding Eckhart Tolle: The Power of Living in The Now

https://www.amazon.com/dp/B078YT86SX

C O N T E N T
(Each step comes with a practical exercise)

UNDERSTANDING ECKHART TOLLE
The Power of Living in the Now
(2 Workbooks in 1)

A. J.   P A R R

WORKBOOK 1

THE SECRET OF NOW SERIES

LIVING IN THE NOW

IN EASY STEPS

A.J. PARR

FOREWORD

ABOUT THIS WORKBOOK

"In essence there is and always has been only one spiritual teaching, although it comes in many forms".

Eckhart Tolle

A. J. PARR

THESE PAGES CONTAIN seven basic lessons and exercises you can easily apply to help you stop your *chattering mind* and begin to experience the Now, a practice that can grant you inner peace and joy STARTING TODAY!

You are about to learn the basic principles and methods behind the ancient practice of *Living in the Now*, the priceless basis of the world's oldest spiritual teachings, including those of Jesus, Buddha, Krishna, Lao Tzu, Kabir, and more recently those of Eckhart Tolle, Krishnamurti, Dalai Lama, Ramana Maharshi, Maharishi Mahesh Yogi, Alan Watts, and countless other renowned teachers.

The seven lessons and exercises you will find in this book are based on the following ancestral premises:

> *Human suffering and unhappiness are produced by our *"chattering mind,"* which unceasingly produces an inner dialogue or chatter, preventing us from experiencing the Now.

> *There is a way to slow down and stop our chattering mind. Once you learn how to do this, you too will be able to slow down and stop it when needed (especially when you sincerely need to stop it and end your distress and self-inflicted suffering.

5

*You cannot stop your thoughts completely, nor is it desirable. Even enlightened beings need to live and interact with society, like all humans.

*By slowing down your chattering mind, you can make them lose their power. Simply recognize them as *"illusions,"* that is, products of a psychological phenomenon common among humans and allegedly known in India since prehistoric times: the phenomenon of mental illusion caused by what for thousands of years has been known as *"the veil of Maya."*

*Only by breaking yourself free from this mental veil you can gradually awaken and free yourself from the psychological illusion that causes human suffering and unhappiness, opening the doors of your inner peace and discovering the joy of Living in the Now!

THE ANCIENT SPIRITUAL WAY OR PATH

One of the facts that most impressed me during my 30 years of Comparative Religion research is that the world's most important religions did not start out as religions but as what their ancient founders called *spiritual paths*. Surprisingly, Jesus, Buddha,

Krishna, Lao-Tse, and Kabir, among other ancient founders of religions, each described his particular teachings as the *"Way"* or *"Path"* in spite of living in very different times and places, as we shall see:

*The oldest religion in the world, presently known as Hinduism, which´s ancestral pre-Vedic roots allegedly date back to the late Stone Age, was originally known as *Sanathana Dharma* or *Perennial Way*.

Around 2,500 years ago Buddha ("Awakened One"* in Sanskrit) also centered his spiritual teachings on the *Dharma* or *Way*, borrowing the Sanskrit term from the Hindus, often defined as the *Way or Path to Awakening or Enlightenment*.

*At least two other ancient world religions derived from Hinduism also adopted the term *Dharma* or *Way*, including Sikhism founded by Guru Nanak (15th Century AD) and Jainism.

*The ancient Chinese based their main philosophies and religions on the concept of what they called the *Tao* (also known as *Dao*), translated as the *"Way"* or *"Path,"* basis of the Taoist teachings of Lao-Tze (6ᵗʰ Century BC).

*The Islamic order of the *Sufis*, the mystical or esoteric branch of Islam officially founded by the prophet Muhammad (7th Century AD) is commonly described as *"the Pathway to Allah."*

*Similarly, according to the *Book of Genesis*, Abraham and the first Prophets of Israel practiced the *Way of the Lord* or *Way of God*, later kept hidden from the masses and which, according to esoteric tradition, served as fundamental basis of the millenary secret teachings of the Temple, from which later derived the *Kabala*, also known as the *Path of Kabbala.*

*Last but not least, the primitive disciples of Jesus and the apostles (years before receiving the name of *Christians*) were originally known, among other names, as *the sect of the Way*, as evidenced in *Acts 9*, among other scriptural testimonies:

"Meanwhile, Saul was still breathing out murderous threats against the Lord's

disciples. He went to the high priest and asked him for letters to the synagogues in Damascus, so that if he found any there who belonged to the Way, whether men or women, he might take them as prisoners to Jerusalem."

THE ART OF LIVING: A THREE-STEP PATH

I have always liked the way the German psychoanalyst Eric Fromm describes the basic steps of learning the *Art of Living* in his best-selling book "*The Art of Loving*":

> *"The first step to take is to become aware that love is an art, just as living is an art. If we want to learn how to love we must proceed in the same way we have to proceed if we want to learn any other art, say music, painting, carpentry, or the art of medicine or engineering.*

> *"What are the necessary steps in learning any art? The process of learning an art can be divided conveniently into two parts: one, the mastery of the theory; the other, the mastery of the practice. If I want to learn the art of medicine, I must first know the facts about the human body, and about various*

diseases. When I have all this theoretical knowledge, I am by no means competent in the art of medicine.

"I shall become a master in this art only after a great deal of practice, until eventually the results of my theoretical knowledge and the results of my practice are blended into one—my intuition, the essence of the mastery of any art."

For practical reasons, in accordance with the ancient spiritual paths of Hinduism and Buddhism, I have divided the *Path* described in these lessons and exercises in the following three different Levels or Stages:

*LEVEL 1: THE APPRENTICE

The new student first learns the basic theory, including that all our problems and sufferings are produced by our own mind, blinded by a veil of delusion that prevents us from experiencing the Now as well as reality "as is." In this initial level, together with the basic theory, the student learns the first exercises that will eventually allow him to develop his "inner eye" and become what is known as the silent Observer. The goal of this initial practice is to recognize the illusory nature of our "chattering mind" and begin to slow down its ever-flowing chain of thoughts.

*LEVEL 2: THE PRACTITIONER

After learning the basic theory and exercises, the student concentrates on practice, for only practice leads to mastery. *By adopting the state of the silent Observer and practicing the art of being Present in the Now (Mindfulness), the student begins to experience brief glimpses of "inner silence and stillness." With practice comes understanding and then the "illusory nature of his ego or false self" is revealed as well as the real essence of his true and transcendental inner Self. It does not depend on intellectual knowledge nor on our understanding or reasoning. It is a direct experience, free of illusion, also described as an awakening. So we mustn't try to grasp it with our minds nor try to understand it, for Inner Peace is a wordless experience that can only be attained here and now in total silence and inner stillness. As the student advances, he or she develops a natural state of* *"renunciation" or "detachment" from the "world of illusion." Hindus call this stage in life **Samnyasa**, which in Sanskrit means "renunciation" or "abandonment."*

*LEVEL 3: THE MASTER

With due knowledge and sufficient practice always comes Mastery. Once the practitioner masters the ancient art of Being Present in the Now, the inner Self or Being gradually surges from within and can be personally felt –though never understood intellectually. When practicing the silent Art of Being Present, advanced practitioners may experience occasional "altered states of consciousness" as well as "non-dual states of consciousness." Known in Hinduism as "Savikalpa Samadhi," these altered states of consciousness are often described as states of "Beingness," that is, of "being aware of one's existence without thinking," characterized by bliss (ananda) and joy (sukha). This process implies regaining awareness of our inner Being and being continuously Present in the Now, enjoying an internalized state of awareness and inner peace often described as "awakened consciousness" or "enlightenment."

And now let's examine these three stages, one by one!

<u>OM LEAD US</u>

Om, Lead us from Illusion
Lead us from Darkness to Light
Lead us from the Fear of Death,
to the Knowledge of Immortality.
Om Peace, Peace, Peace!

(Brihadaranyaka Upanishad)

* * *

14

FIRST LEVEL:

THE APPRENTICE

Introductory Teachings and Training

The new student first learns the basic theory, including that all our problems and sufferings are produced by our own mind, blinded by a veil of delusion that prevents us from experiencing the Now as well as reality "as is". In this initial level, together with the basic theory, the student learns the first exercises that will eventually allow him to develop his "inner eye" and become what is known as the silent Observer. The goal of this initial practice is to recognize the illusory nature of our "chattering mind" and begin to slow down its ever-flowing chain of thoughts.

LESSON 1

THE VEIL OF DELUSION

"Man, because he sacrifices his health in order to make money. Then he sacrifices money to recuperate his health. And then he is so anxious about the future that he does not enjoy the present; the result being that he does not live in the present or the future; he lives as if he is never going to die, and then he dies having never really lived."

Dalai Lama

17

THIS LESSON MARKS THE START of your Spiritual Journey to a better, healthier life, and a clear understanding that your problems, unhappiness, and suffering are not caused by specific situations in your life but by "your illusory thoughts about them", that is, by "what you, in your own head, tell yourself about them".

Truth is, thanks to reason and logic, you have given birth to an imaginary World of Illusion that only exists in your mind. It is your subjective interpretation of the world from your personal perspective. A mental image, as we shall see that has replaced the real world in your mind, created and nurtured by your own thoughts, beliefs, values, and judgments.

THE ANCIENT TEACHING OF MAYA

The ancient Hindu word *Maya* comes from the Sanskrit roots *"ma"* ("not") and *"ya"* ("that"), literally meaning *"not that"* or *"that which is not that"*, loosely meaning "Illusion".

As Eckhart explains, ancient Hindus represented this self-created illusion as *the veil of Maya,* a symbolic veil or curtain that distorts reality and makes humans chase vain dreams like madmen.

People do all sorts of things due to Maya´s veil of delusion:

*They are always chasing new desires and illusory –therefore unreachable- goals.

*They always imagine a better future and the more they think about it, the more they feel unsatisfied with their present lives.

*Also they are always remembering and reliving s better or worse past moments and are therefore unable to experience the Now.

*They are always comparing themselves with others and complaining about their "unsatisfactory" achievements.

*They live a "false life," ruled by a "fake self-image," believing "they are someone they´re not."

*They are always deceiving each other, unknowingly or not, as well as themselves.

Why do they do this?

Because of the golden veil of *Maya,* which distorts and blurs our vision, preventing us from "seeing" our true Nature and experiencing our true Self as well as profound inner peace.

THE MIND IS MAYA

One of India´s most celebrated gurus of all times, Ramana Maharshi (1879–1950), once summed up the essence of the spiritual teachings of Hinduism in four simple words:

"The mind is Maya."

According to him, Maya can "possess" and sink us in a dream-like state, making us chase illusions in vain. It can also make us believe we are someone we are not, forget our spiritual duties, create unhappy using our own mechanical thoughts.

To understand the dream-like state created by Maya, the Hindu sage Swami Vivekananda (1863-1902) told the following tale about young Narada, one of the dearest disciples of the Hindu spiritual master Lord Krishna:

A. J. PARR

KRISHNA AND THE DREAM OF MAYA

Ramana Maharshi

I.

One day, as they walked through the woods, Krishna told his young disciple Narada about Maya and the veil of delusion.

"All you can think about all you see, Narada, is only an Illusion created by the veil of Maya" Krishna explained as they walked.

"I see what you mean, dear Master, but it´s so hard to understand," said the young chela. *"How can everything we think about everything be false?*

"You will understand it the day you experience the Power of Maya, my child," said Krishna.

"My Lord, I want to understand," Narada said and then asked his master with his characteristic wide smile: *"Can you show me now the Power of Maya?"*

Krishna looked at the young chela thoughtfully and raised an eyebrow.

But he did not reply.

II.

A few days passed, and Krishna asked Narada to travel with him to the desert.

After walking for several miles under the intense sun, Krishna told him:

"I´m thirsty, Narada. Can you get me some water?"

"Yes, Master. I saw a small village nearby. I will go there at once and bring you some water" said the young disciple eagerly walking away with quick steps.

He knew exactly where to go.

III.

Narada entered the village in search of water. Almost immediately, one of the biggest houses powerfully drew his attention.

After knocking on the door, a most beautiful young girl opened it and stepped out with a smile.

It was the most beautiful woman Narada had ever seen!

As soon as he saw her, the young disciple he drew his characteristic broad smile on his face and immediately forgot that his Master was thirsty and waiting for his water.

The young disciple spent the rest of that day with the girl. And that night he did not return to his dear Master.

The next morning, Narada went to see her again, and they spent the whole day together, chatting and walking across her father's fields. But all that talking quickly ripened into love.

A few days later he asked her father for her hand, and they got married shortly after.

IV.

Filled with overflowing happiness, Narada made the small village his new home. He found a job administering his father-in-law's farm, bought a little house for him and his wife, and they were soon blessed by children.

25

Twelve years slowly passed by...

Narada wasn't the same man anymore.

His broad, characteristic smile was long gone. Now he was always complaining. He was buried in debts and didn't know what to do! In fact, sometimes he hated his life!

But one day his father-in-law died, and Narada inherited the farm together with a small fortune.

All of the sudden, he had more money than he could spend!

Narada soon recovered his broad smile, as well as his deep love for life. As he seemed to think, he was pleased with his wife, his three children, his fields of crops, his numerous heads of cattle and his small fortune.

He had more than he had ever dreamed!

Everything seemed perfect!

But everything was about to change by a sudden twist of fate...

V.

One night, unexpectedly, there was a tragic flood.

It was past midnight when the village river waters rose without notice and overflowed its banks, flooding the place in the middle of the night.

It was a real tragedy!

Houses fell, many people and animals drowned, and half the village was swept away by the rush of the brutal stream.

Suddenly Narada found he trapped in his battered home, surrounded by raging waters, together with his dear wife and children.

Their house began to shake. It was about to fall in on them!

They needed to escape!

Standing by the open door, Narada held his dear wife with one hand, and with the other, he grabbed two of his children. His third child, the smallest of the three, jumped fast on his shoulders.

Narada looked out the door and saw the rushing waters.

It seemed more than he could take.

But he had no choice.

Ready or not, he was about to meet his fate.

Narada stepped out the door holding his family close. But as soon as he took a few steps in the water, he found the current was too strong!

The waters struck wildly against them!

Narada stumbled and, all of the sudden, the child on his shoulders fell off and was swept away!

Narada shot a cry of despair!

Trying to grab and save his young son, he stretched out his hand instinctively... But by doing so, he let go of his other two children, who were immediately carried away and the three sank in the mighty current!

Narada cried out in deep pain!

He embraced his dear wife with all his might. She was all he had left!

But the current was too strong, and suddenly his wife was also torn away from him and was carried away by the mighty waters in which she sank!

He too was swept by the mighty current. He thought it was the end. Only then he remembered his dear Master Krishna. But it was too late.

VI.

Almost unconscious, Narada sank and twirled beneath the torrential waters, only to be surprisingly hurled with great force onto the riverbank!

Narada was alive!

But his pain was too intense. Weeping and wailing in bitter lamentation, he wished he was dead!

Suddenly, from behind him, there came a gentle voice: "My child, Narada. Where is my water?"

Narada turned around and was amazed to see Krishna smiling at him.

"Where is my water?" his Master repeated. "You went for water half an hour ago! And I'm still waiting!

Narada looked around dumbfounded.

The rough waters, the torn buildings, the few trees that were still left standing, and even the river and its bank... Everything had vanished!

"Did you say half an hour ago, Master?" Narada asked Krishna, scratching his head.

Everything seemed so unreal!

"Of course, Narada! You were only gone for half an hour!"

Narada couldn't believe it!

Twelve whole years had passed by, but only in his mind! All in half an hour!

All he lived in those twelve years, all those days and experiences, all those joys and sorrows, all those weeks, months and years... Everything had only been an Illusion!

"Yes, my child. It's just what you asked for, isn't it?" Krishna gently asked, placing a paternal hand on Narada's shoulder. "Now you know the Power of Maya!"

FIRST EXERCISE

OBSERVING YOUR THOUGHTS

"Try a little experiment. Close your eyes and say to yourself: 'I wonder what my next thought is going to be.' Then become very alert and wait for the next thought. Be like a cat watching a mouse hole. What thought is going to come out of the mouse hole? Try it now."

Eckhart Tolle

31

THE FOLLOWING EXERCISE WILL SHOW YOU how to "Observe your thoughts," a basic step in understanding the basics of "conscious thinking" and how the veil of delusion affects us.

Remember what Eckhart recommends:

"To free yourself from Illusion and experience spiritual growth, you must become the Observer."

You can practice this exercise by yourself, as well as the rest of the exercises contained in this book. However, it's better if you have someone else with you the first time you practice. This way he or she can read out the instructions as you exercise. Great practice for couples!

OBSERVING YOUR THOUGHTS

This exercise will prepare you for the rest of the drills contained in this workbook, specially designed to boost your spiritual growth.

To get started just follow these steps:

1:

This exercise will last less than a minute. Sit or lie down in a comfortable and relaxing position. The position you now have while reading this book will do. You can also adopt another or a meditation or yoga pose.

2:

Close your eyes. Although you can do this exercise with your eyes open, I recommend closing them this first time to avoid unwanted distractions and increase your concentration.

3:

No matter what you think when you close your eyes, this will be your thought number one. Remember this.

For example, you may be thinking "I wonder what this exercise is all about" or "I'm hungry" or "Hey! I forgot to call mom!" What you're thinking doesn't matter. Above all, here's what you need to do:

*Realize that you are having a thought.

*Recognize your thought, that is, understand what the thought is all about. For example: "I need to go to the bank tomorrow."

4:

Once you "get the idea" or "understand your though" say "YES!" out loud.

Apart from forcing you to keep focused on the exercise, saying it out loud will also help you interrupt your thinking process briefly, which is the primary purpose of the following step.

5:

If the information is important, like for example having to go to the bank tomorrow, take mental note and leave it for later. If it is not, then ignore it. In either case, to stop thinking about it jump to the next step.

6:

Immediately say to yourself, following Eckhart´s instructions:

"I wonder what my next thought is going to be."

Be alert. Watch your mind. Wait for your next thought.

Like Eckhart says, "be like a cat watching a mouse hole."

7:

Very soon you will think about something, or a new thought will spontaneously pop in your head. Either way, it fine.

Identify your new thought. For example: "I´m thirsty" or "What was the name of that person I met yesterday?" For the sake of this experiment, this will be your "thought number two."

8:

Don´t engage in your thought. Simply be alert and recognize it. As soon as you know what your "thought number two" is about, say "YES!" out loud. This will help you interrupt your "chain of thoughts" and continue with the next step.

9:

After saying "yes," stop thinking about it. Leave it for later and let it go. Try putting your mind in "blank" and continue to the next step.

10:

Once again, follow Eckhart's instructions and mentally say to yourself:

"I wonder what my next thought is going to be."

You don't need to say this verbally, only if you want to. Just be alert and wait for your next thought. *"Be like a cat watching a mouse hole."*

11:

Soon a third thought will arise. It doesn't matter if it is "Where did I leave my keys?" or "I'm sleepy" or "I'm having thoughts." Just be alert and silently recognize your new thought as soon as it appears.

The co-founder of the Chopra Center, Dr. David Simon, an expert in transcendental meditation, often told his students:

"The thought *I'm having thoughts* may be the most important thought you have ever thought, because before you had that thought, you may not have even known you were having thoughts. You probably thought you *were* your thoughts."

12:

As soon as you recognize your third thought and identify what it's about, say "YES" one last time before taking a deep breath and opening your eyes.

13:

Repeat this exercise two or three times a day - observing only three thoughts each time will do. It will take you less than half a minute. Just remember: after recognizing each new thought and saying "YES!", immediately leave it for later and stop thinking about it.

Apart from allowing you to "observe your thoughts" this excrcise also teaches you how to let your thoughts go. And I cannot express how important this is when trying to slow down and stop your "unceasing mental chatter."

As you will experience in the following exercises, learning to "release" your thoughts will help you avoid engaging in an endless monologue or a mental discussion with no end and give yourself a break. And don't forget the primary purpose of these first set of exercises:

"Be present. Be there as the Observer of the mind."

LESSON 2

THE DUAL NATURE OF MAYA

"There exists only the present instant... a Now which always and without end is itself new. There is no yesterday nor any tomorrow, but only Now, as it was a thousand years ago and as it will be a thousand years hence..."

Meister Eckhart

MAYA IS THE ANCIENT SANSKRIT WORD for thousands of years used to describe *"the state of mind in which we are prevented from experiencing our true Self or Ultimate Reality,"* or *"the primary phenomenon that prevents us from attaining enlightenment and realizing the true nature of all things."* It is also the name of the Hindu goddess *Maya* or *MahaMaya, the ancient Mother of Illusion,* dreams, deceptions, and spells, which she manifests, perpetuates and governs at will. According to olden Hindu tradition, this goddess has two opposite natures: a lower or negative one and a higher or positive. Let's take a quick look at both of them:

THE LOWER NATURE OF MAYA

According to Hindu tradition, the goddess Maya is capable of tempting and captivating even the strongest man. And once she has him under her control, she reveals "her true evil form." Truth is, most people are permanently experiencing the lower essence of *Maya,* that is, her dreaded "veil of delusion."

Known as "the deceiver" or the "secret enemy," this lower essence of *Maya* can trap you in an imaginary dream-like state, just like the one Krishna's disciple, young Narada had when he experienced twelve years in only half an hour, as told in the first lesson.

This dream-like state, comparable to madness, is produced by our imaginary beliefs, values, joys, and sorrows. Fact is, just like Narada, most of us live "imaginary lives" and, without realizing it, we vainly chase empty dreams and illusory goals; always imagining a better future or remembering a better past, and always complaining about the Now.

Also like Narada, most people end up believing we are "someone we are not," assuming false identities. We say "I am this" or "I am that." But in reality, due to the veil of Maya, most of us don't even know who or what we truly are!

THE HIGHER NATURE OF MAYA

According to Hindu teachings, the higher nature of *Maya* has a "positive" and "transcendental" purpose, for it serves us as "spiritual teacher" and "giver of superior knowledge."

As experience shows, "deception often leads to the truth." This is why in Hindu tradition the goddess Maya is also known as the "giver of awareness" and "bringer of evolution." Its higher essence, instead of sinking you deeper into the world of illusion, can actually help you "wake up from the dream" and reach the road to enlightenment.

How?

Find out by reading the following pages!

AND THIS IS MĀYĀ

Swami Vivekananda

Hope is dominant in the heart of childhood. The whole world is a golden vision to the opening eyes of the child; he thinks his will is supreme. As he moves onward, at every step nature stands as an adamantine wall, barring his future progress. He may hurl himself against it, again and again, striving to break through. But the further he goes, the further recedes the ideal, till death comes, and there is release, perhaps. **And this is Maya.**

The senses drag the human soul out. Man is seeking for pleasure and for happiness where it can never be found. For countless ages we are all taught that this is futile and vain, there is no happiness here. But we cannot learn; it is impossible for us to do so, except through our own experiences. We try them, and a blow comes. Do we learn then? Not even then. Like moths hurling themselves against the flame, we are hurling ourselves again and again into sense-pleasures, hoping to find satisfaction there. We

41

*return again and again with freshened energy; thus we go on, till crippled and cheated we die. **And this is Maya.***

*So with our intellect. In our desire to solve the mysteries of the universe, we cannot stop our questioning; we feel we must know and cannot believe that no knowledge is to be gained. A few steps, and there arises the wall of beginningless and endless time which we cannot surmount. A few steps, and there appears a wall of boundless space which cannot be conquered, and the whole is irrevocably bound in by the walls of cause and effect. We cannot go beyond them. Yet we struggle, and still have to struggle. **And this is Maya.***

*With every breath, with every pulsation of the heart with every one of our movements, we think we are free, and the very same moment we are shown that we are not. Bound slaves, nature's bond-slaves, in body, in mind, in all our thoughts, in all our feelings. **And this is Maya.***

(Public speech delivered in London, 22 October 1896)

* * *

SECOND EXERCISE

COUNTING YOUR THOUGHTS

"You have probably come across 'mad' people in the street incessantly talking or muttering to themselves. Well, that's not much different from what you and all other "normal" people do, except that you don't do it out loud."

Eckhart Tolle

ACCORDING TO ECKHART TOLLE, we cannot experience the Power of Now unless we learn to stop our unceasing "mental dialogue or chatter":

*A chatter that is always about the past or about the future, but hardly about the present.

*A chatter that always distracts you and always triggers more thoughts.

*A chatter that prevents you from experiencing the "Now"!

Unfortunately, most people are unaware of this. But how on earth can they be aware of it if they're always too busy, endlessly speaking in their minds?

COUNTING YOUR THOUGHTS:

Minute by minute, hour by hour, and day by day, your "mental chatter" sinks you more profound into the illusory world of Maya. The following exercise will allow you to calculate how many involuntary thoughts you have in a minute or so.

You will need the following:

*A calculator.

*A stopwatch or something to keep track of time.

Someone to assist you, mainly so he or she can keep track of the time while you concentrate on the exercise. You can also take turns if you want.

PART ONE OF THE EXERCISE

1:

Sit or lie down in a comfortable and relaxing position. The position you now have while reading this book will do, or use a meditation or yoga pose if you like.

2:

Close your eyes. You can do this exercise with your eyes open, but with eyes closed, you will avoid distractions and increase concentration.

3:

No matter what you're thinking about when you close your eyes, that will be your "thought number one," just like in our last exercise.

For example, you may be thinking "I wonder what this exercise is all about" or "I'm hungry" or "Wow! I forgot to call mom!" That will be your thought number one. What you're thinking doesn't matter. Above all, don't get involved with your thought, that is, do not turn a single thought into a "conversation" or "monologue." Simply do the following:

*Realize that you are having a thought now, in the present moment.

*Be aware of the moment. Recognize your thought, that is, understand what the thought is all about. For example: "I need to go to the bank tomorrow."

4:

Once you recognize your though, say out loud or yell out the word "ONE!" (The number of the thought).

5:

Don´t engage in your thought. Recognize it, take mental note if needed, leave it for later, let it go and jump to the next step.

6:

Be alert and wait for your next thought. "Be like a cat watching a mouse hole," as Eckhart recommends. Very soon a new thought will pop into your head. This will be your "thought number two." As soon as it appears, recognize it and say "TWO!" (The number of the second thought). Immediately after saying this, stop thinking about it, leave it for later, and let it go.

7:

Continue repeating the process for precisely 60 seconds (a full minute). No less, not more.

REMEMBER:

*Each time a new idea appears, repeat the process: recognize it, say its number and let it go.

*Don't get engaged in your thoughts during the exercise.

*Keep track of the number of thoughts you have by saying each number out loud.

*When the 60 seconds are up, write down the total number.

For example: 25 thoughts (that was my result the first time I did this exercise).

PART TWO OF THE EXERCISE

Take out your calculator, a notebook or blank paper and a pencil or pen (You can also use your computer or laptop instead).

*YOUR PER-MINUTE RATE:

Write down the number of thoughts you had in 60 seconds (one minute).

This number is what we´re really after in the first part of this exercise. It will tell you, approximately, your THOUGHTS PER MINUTE or TPM RATE. For example, my TPM rate the first time I did this exercise was 25 thoughts per minute.

What´s your TPM rate?

*YOUR PER- HOUR RATE:

Suppose you had 25 thoughts, as I did. Take that number and multiply it by 60.This will let you know your approximate THOUGHTS PER HOUR OR TPH RATE. In my case, it was 25 x 60.

That's 1,500 thoughts per hour!

What's your TPH rate?

*YOUR PER-DAY RATE:

To calculate how many thoughts you have in a single day, multiply your TPH times 24. That WILL BE YOUR THOUGHTS PER DAY or TPD RATE.

For example, in my case, 1,500 times 24.

This gave me a total of 36,000 thoughts per day!

What's your TPD rate?

*YOUR PER-YEAR RATE:

Finally, multiply your TPD RATE by 365, and that will give you your approximate THOUGHTS PER YEAR or TPY RATE. In my case, 36,000 times 365.

THAT'S OVER 13 MILLION THOUGHTS IN A YEAR!

*13,140,000 thoughts per year to be exact.

*There are 525,600 minutes in a year.

*How many of these thoughts made me feel good? How many made me feel bad? How many were useful? How many were a waste of time? How many gave me inner peace and how many stressed me out? How many helped me in my Spiritual Journey and how many sank me even deeper into the world of Illusion?

And you? What´s your TPY rate?

Like I mentioned, doing this exercise allows you to measure the approximate rate of your "unceasing inner chat," which minute by minute, hour by hour, and day by day, sinks you deeper and deeper in the illusory world of Maya ...*unless you decide to do something about it!*

LESSON 3

THE CHATTERING MIND

"I am just asking you why does the mind chatter? Is it a habit or does the mind need to be occupied with something? And when it is not occupied with what it thinks it should be occupied, we call it chattering. Why should not the occupation be chattering also? I am occupied with my house. You are occupied with your God, with your work, with your business, with your wife, with your sex, with your children, with your property. The mind needs to be occupied with something, and therefore when it is not occupied, it may feel a sense of emptiness and therefore chatters."

Krishnamurti

A. J.   P A R R

ACCORDING TO AN ANCIENT SAYING, if you cannot control your own mind, then your mind is actually controlling you! And that's a problem you can't afford!

The reason for not being able to control our minds is that most people are unconsciously identified with their "inner voice" and are unknowing "slaves" of their own automatic or programmed thoughts, beliefs, values, and desires.

The Indian philosopher Jiddu Krishnamurti (1895-1986) usually referred to the thinking mind as the *"chattering mind,"* stating that this chatter is a constant process, an endless operation, and that *"every moment it is murmuring."*

In his 1954 best-seller *"The First and Last Freedom"* he stated:

> *"As I watch the brain, I see that the chattering happens only in the brain, it is a brain activity; a current flows up and down, but it is chaotic, meaningless and purposeless. The brain wears itself out by its own activity. One can see that it is tiring to the brain, but it does not stop... The mind chatters all the time, and the energy devoted to that purpose fills a major part of our life.*

> *"The mind apparently needs to be occupied with something... The mind is occupied with something, and if it is not occupied, it feels*

vacant, it feels empty, and therefore it resorts to chattering..."

Regarding the need to quiet our chattering mind and acquire the silent state of inner stillness, Krishnamurti stated:

"The still mind is the most active mind, but if you experiment with it, go into it deeply, you will see that in stillness there is no projection of thought. Thought, at all levels, is obviously the reaction of memory, and thought can never be in a state of creation. It may express creativeness, but thought in itself can never be creative. When there is silence - that tranquility of mind which is not a result - then we shall see that in that quietness there is extraordinary activity, an extraordinary action which a mind agitated by thought can never know...

"The still mind is the most active mind, but if you experiment with it, go into it deeply, you will see that in stillness there is no projection of thought. Thought, at all levels, is obviously the reaction of memory and thought can never be in a state of creation. It may express creativeness but thought in itself can never be creative. When there is silence, that tranquillity of mind which is

not a result, then we shall see that in that quietness there is extraordinary activity, an extraordinary action which a mind agitated by thought can never know.

Only by observing yourself in complete stillness you will be able to actually "see" who you really are. This is why all the ancient wise men of Athens highlighted the importance of the olden maxim inscribed in the Temple of Apollo in the city of Delphi: *"Know thyself."*

That's basically it: You must know yourself! And the best way to do this, as you will see in the following lessons, is through Self-observation, that is, by recognizing your own thoughts and learning how to slow them down and experience "inner stillness."

Remember; No one else can do this for you. Only you can!

In conclusion, to attain spiritual progress you merely need to practice and follow your heart. Simply experience things for yourself. And please don't pay attention to other people's opinions, beliefs, values, and desires.

In this early stage of your spiritual training, you first need to concentrate on observing the voice in your head until you are finally fit to grab the reins of your life and experience inner peace and happiness for yourself!

* * *

THE SILENT LANGUAGE

Silence is ever-speaking,

It is the perennial flow of "language."

It is interrupted by speaking,

For words destroy this mute language.

Silence is unceasing eloquence.

It is the best language.

There is a state when words cease

And silence prevails.

* * *

THIRD EXERCISE

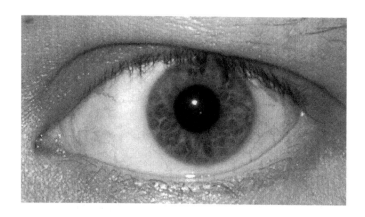

AWAKENING THE SILENT OBSERVER

"Start listening to the voice in your head as often as you can. Pay particular attention to any repetitive thought patterns, those old gramophone records that have been playing in your head perhaps for many years. This is what I mean by "watching the thinker," which is another way of saying: listen to the voice in your head, be there as the witnessing presence.

"When you listen to that voice, listen to it impartially. That is to say, do not judge. Do not judge or condemn what you hear, for doing so would mean that the same voice has come in again through the back door. You'll soon realize: there is the voice, and here I am listening to it, watching it. This 'I am' realization, this sense of your own presence, is not a thought. It arises from beyond the mind..."

Eckhart Tolle

THE DEVELOPMENT OF YOUR INNER VISION or insight is fundamental if you seek to free yourself from the heavy load of your daily problems. As these pages evidence, most of your personal problems are *"self-inflicted,"* that is, they are illusory creations of your own mind.

In his book *"Transcendent Wisdom,"* the Dalai Lama explains that one of the basic aspects of Tibetan philosophy derives from the ancient teachings of the celebrated 8th-century monk known as Shantideva, who stated that human beings experience two basic and distinctive realities:

ILLUSORY REALITY:

The first and most commonly perceived is called *"conventional reality"* or *"illusory reality"* and is basically a production or projection of our own mind or intellect. It can be described as a personal and relative view of the world based on duality and our own speculations and ideas of what this reality should be. In sum, it is only the product of our own imagination!

Illusory reality only exists within our own minds. It is like a dream or the trick of a magician, as the Dalai Lama warns in *"Transcendent Wisdom"*:

> *"While dreaming, all kinds of things may come to mind, but these are nothing more than appearances. Likewise, a magician may*

create a variety of illusory appearances, but they do not exist objectively..."

REAL REALITY:

The second is subjacent and known as *"ultimate reality"* or *"real reality."* It is everything that truly exists. It cannot be perceived by the intellect nor described in words, and can only be directly experienced by seekers of the Path who have effectively *"tamed"* their minds and developed their *"inner sight"* or *"third eye."*

FREEING YOURSELF FROM ILLUSION

Unless we learn to recognize the falseness of our own illusory world, it will continue deceiving and sinking us in a world of suffering and hostility.

As the Dalai Lama preaches, to free ourselves from the chains of illusion, we must first learn to perceive reality as the only Truth. This Truth is often referred to in ancient Buddhist scriptures as *"emptiness"* because it cannot be described with words other than "void of form, name, shape, characteristics and beyond time and space."

Also according to the Dalai Lama, unless we experience this true reality within us, within our hearts, and stop believing in the world of verbal thinking and all the mental representations we have erected within our heads, we will inexorably continue to be blinded by the veil of illusion woven by our own ignorance. An illusion that always brings new joys and satisfactions that are always followed by further suffering and dissatisfaction, endlessly turning like a spinning wheel that intimately affects the outcome of our daily living and very often disturbs our general wellbeing.

Recognizing and experiencing *"real reality,"* as the Dalai Lama states, is the only way of freeing ourselves from the heavy chains of illusion that cause our suffering. And once we do this, we will recognize our *"illusory reality"* as a foul dream that is not real and only then it will cease to affect our natural state of perpetual happiness and wellbeing.

OPENING THE INNER EYE

Truth is, for thousands of years the *"inner eye,"* also known as the *"eye of the soul,"* has been widely studied in India, including the followers of both Hinduism and Buddhism. But it is also said that Jesus openly referred to it in Matthew 6:22-23:

> *"The light of the body is the eye, therefore when your eye is good, your whole body is full of light; but when your eye is bad, your body is full of darkness. Take heed therefore that the light which is in you be not darkness. If thy whole body is therefore full of light, having no part dark, the whole shall be full of*

light, as when the bright shining of a candle does give you light."

According to the ancient teachings of Hinduism and Buddhism, the third eye is located in the middle of the forehead and is the gate to *"the inner realms and higher states of consciousness."* Hindu tradition associates the third eye with the *ajna*, or the chakra of the brow.

AWAKENING THE OBSERVER

Awakening the Observer or Silent Witness is a vital step when learning to tame the mind and is the object of the present exercise. It will allow you to recognize "the voice in your head" as something different from your true Self.

To begin to awaken your inner eye and adopt the state of the just follow these steps:

1:

Sit or lie down in a comfortable and relaxing position. The position you now have while reading this book will do, or use a meditation or yoga pose if you like.

2:

Close your eyes. No matter what you're thinking, realize that you are having a thought and identify it. Once you recognize it, say "yes" out loud and, without engaging in your thought, leave it for later and let it go as you learned to do in the last exercises.

3:

Try to keep complete mental silence for a second or two. Simple be alert and wait for your next thought. "Be like a cat watching a mouse hole," as Eckhart explains. Keep mentally silent and wait for "the voice in your head" to say something new, something spontaneous, that is, on its own and without you voluntarily participating.

4:

Very soon, despite your silence, you will hear the "voice in your head" say something new, as if it had "a will of its own." Immediately try to identify the two distinctive players that are participating within your head:

*The voice in your head.

*And you as the silent observer.

To help you identify the two players, Eckhart recommends asking yourself: "Am I the thoughts that are going through my head? Or, am I the one who is aware that these thoughts are going through my head?"

5:

Recognize the new thought before saying "yes" out loud and, without engaging in your thought, leave it for later and let it go. Repeat the process several times until you begin to experience the separation between the "voice in your head" (which uses verbal language) and you as the Observer (immersed in silence).

Remember, let "the voice in your head" do the talking. Don't try to control it. Simply observe your mind in silence. As soon as a new idea appears, recognize it, say "yes" and let it go.

Remember:

Try to experience being the Observer, don't get engaged in your thoughts during the exercise, and prepare yourself to begin the second level of our Spiritual Journey!

SECOND LEVEL

THE PRACTITIONER

The Practice of Observing Presence

After learning the basic theory and exercises, the student concentrates on practice, for only practice leads to mastery. By adopting the state of the silent Observer and practicing the art of being Present in the Now (Mindfulness), the student begins to experience brief glimpses of "inner silence and stillness." With practice comes understanding and then the "illusory nature of his ego or false self" is revealed as well as the real essence of his true and transcendental inner Self. It does not depend on intellectual knowledge nor our understanding or reasoning. It is a direct experience, free of illusion, also described as an awakening. So we mustn't try to grasp it with our minds nor try to understand it, for Inner Peace is a wordless experience that can only be attained here and now in total silence and inner stillness. As the student *advances, he or she develops a natural state of "renunciation" or "detachment" from the "world of illusion." Hindus call this stage in life* **Samnyasa,** *which in Sanskrit means "renunciation" or "abandonment."*

LESSON 4

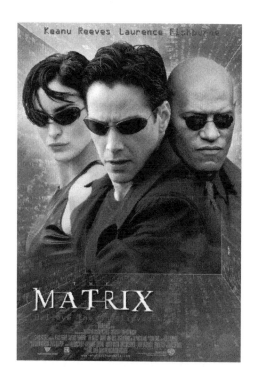

THE NATURE OF THE EGO AND THE SELF

"I'm trying to free your mind, Neo. But I can only show you the door. You're the one that has to walk through it... There is a difference between knowing the path and walking the path."

Morpheus – The Matrix

A. J.   P A R R

IN THE CELEBRATED FILM *MATRIX* (1999), Thomas A. Anderson is a skillful computer expert living two lives: By day he is an ordinary computer programmer. But by night he is a secret hacker known as Neo.

Neo is a rebel. He has always questioned the present. He is unsatisfied with his reality. He needs change. But he never imagined that soon he would find out that everything he had lived in his life was only a dream!

A vain illusion just like Narada's!

This is how Neo´s amazing and futuristic story begins:

> *Neo is contacted by Morpheus, a legendary computer hacker, and a known terrorist. Neo has heard a lot about him. He has always secretly admired him as his superior in age, experience, and wisdom. But he knows Morpheus only means trouble!*

> *Morpheus surprises Neo by suddenly asking him:*

> *"Have you ever had a dream, Neo, that you were so sure was real? What if you were unable to wake from that dream? How would you know*

the difference between the dream-world and the real world?"

Morpheus then tells Neo the world as they know it is only an illusory dream that veils another world.

But Neo refuses to believe it!

To convince him, Morpheus tells him what he calls "the Truth": The "illusion of this world" is a perpetual dream artificially created by an enslaving machine called The Matrix, which feeds on human bio-electricity.

"The Matrix is a computer-generated dream-world built to keep us under control in order to change a human being into this," Morpheus said, holding up a Duracell battery.

"No!" Neo exclaimed shaking his head in denial. "I don't believe it! It's not possible!

"The Matrix is everywhere" Morpheus continued saying. "It is all around us. Even now, in this very room. You can see it when you look out your window or when you turn on your television. You can feel it when you go to work...

when you go to church... when you pay your taxes. It is the world that has been pulled over your eyes to blind you from the truth."

"What truth?" asks Neo.

"That you are a slave, Neo. Like everyone else, you were born into bondage. Into a prison that you cannot taste or see or touch. A prison for your mind."

* * *

Did you notice any similarities between Matrix and the world of Maya? For the purpose of this lesson, I will only point out a couple:

*The false Neo (trapped in the Illusion of the Matrix) can be compared with our "illusory self" or ego.

*The real Neo (free from the Illusion of the Matrix) can be compared with our natural Self.

Having said that, I believe the moral of the symbolic story is quite clear:

Only through Self-knowledge we can escape from the world of Illusion and transcend from ego to Self.

SELF-KNOWLEDGE: THE KEY TO FREEDOM

According to the ancient teachings of Hinduism, to free ourselves from the chains the illusions of this world and attain salvation, first we must acquire Self-knowledge *(atma jnana)*.

But what did they mean by Self-knowledge?

Basically, the knowledge that our true Self or Atman is not our illusory self or ego. And that our true Self is identical with the transcendental Self we call God or Brahman: the Ultimate Reality.

The ancient rishis of Hinduism divided the study of Self-knowledge into two separate branches. But both are really One:

The knowledge of the lower animal self or ego (the psychological "I," the thinker)

The knowledge of the true Self or soul, (the transcendental "I," the Observer)

Since the dawn of humankind, these teaching have been passed down, from Master to disciple, and from generation to generation, and finally, they have reached our present time.

THE KNOWLEDGE OF THE EGO

According to Eckhart Tolle, *"as you grow up, you form a mental image of which you are, based on your personal and cultural conditioning. We may call this phantom self the ego."*

Eckhart's teachings, as well as the Hindu's, claim that your "*ego*" or "*rational mind*" needs constant thinking to exist. People become addicted to thinking because they are identified with their erroneous "*sense of self.*"

Building your ego is like building a castle in your imagination.

The more you think about it, the more details you will imagine and the stronger your mental image of the castle will be. Only that in this case you are the castle.

Don't take it wrong, but you are not who you think you are.

No matter what you think, the "*mental image of who you are*" is only speculation, a supposition, an imaginary you that you have created and that you nurture with your thoughts.

But it is only an illusion!

As I said, you're not who you think you are! The person who you think you are is only a creation of your limited mind, an image you have built since your childhood and in which you have thought all your life!

The more you think about it, the stronger it gets.

The less you think about it, the weaker it gets.

And if you stop thinking about it will reach a dormant state and disappear!

73

When one of his disciples asked the famous nineteenth-century Hindu mystic Ramakrishna what the ego is, the wise man replied:

> *"Ponder deeply, and you will know that there is no such thing as 'I.' As you peel off the skin of an onion, you find it consists only of skin; you cannot find any kernel in it. So too on analyzing the ego, you will find that there is no real entity that you can call 'I.' Such an analysis of the ego convinces one that the ultimate substance is God alone. When egotism drops away, Divinity manifests Itself."*

THE KNOWLEDGE OF THE SELF

Atman in Sanskrit means *"Inner-Self"* or *"soul."*

The Atman is our true Self, beyond identification with phenomena. It is the higher Self, identified with the Absolute Substance or Brahman, the transcendental One, beyond space and time, formless and unchangeable.

Since the ultimate reality is that all is One, then we are all part of the One too, as well as everything that surrounds us (including the whole universe).

The only way for the Absolute to experience "individuality" is through the illusion of the ego, that is, through the power of Maya.

Without Maya, we would not be able to experience separation from the Absolute and would only experience the One. Such is the power of Maya.

But this apparent *"individuality"* or *"separation from the One"* it is only a game or Leela played by the Absolute, our true Self.

According to Hinduism:

The One, or Absolute: Reality, is always real.

It has no form. It has no name.

It is limitless. It is not bound. It is beyond space and time.

It is the formless being which sustains the universe.

It transcends speech and therefore cannot be described.

It is your inner-Self, subjective awareness of "I am."

It is your real form (nija-swarupa).

It dwells in the center of your heart.

* * *

CONFUSED BY THOUGHTS

HUI NENG

Confused by thoughts,

we experience duality in life.

Unencumbered by ideas,

the enlightened see the one Reality.

* * *

FOURTH EXERCISE

EXPERIENCING THE GAP

"The mind is quiet when it sees the truth that understanding comes only when it is quiet. That if I would understand you, I must be quiet, I cannot have reactions against you, I must not be prejudiced, I must put away all my conclusions, my experiences and meet you face to face. Only then, when the mind is free from my conditioning, do I understand. When I see the truth of that, then the mind is quiet - and then there is no question of how to make the mind quiet."

Krishnamurti

ALTHOUGH YOUR CHATTERING MIND unceasingly speaks, generating thousands of thoughts per day, try to detect the brief space between one thought and the next: the silent gap. During these gaps, according to Eckhart, the awareness of something simply becomes the awareness of the Now.

To start experiencing these gaps, just follow the steps:

1:

Sit or lie down in a comfortable and relaxing position. The position you now have while reading this book will do, or use a meditation or yoga pose if you like.

2:

Close your eyes. No matter what you're thinking, realize that you are having a thought and identify it. Once you recognize it, say "YES!" out loud and, without engaging in your first thought, leave it for later and let it go as you learned to do in the last exercises.

3:

Try to keep complete mental silence for a second or two. "Be like a cat watching a mouse hole." Before your new thought arrives, you will experience a brief blank space or gap between your first and second thoughts. It may only last a brief instant.

"Pay attention to the gap," Eckhart Tolle says in his book *Stillness Speaks*, "the gap between two thoughts, the brief, silent space between words in a conversation, between the notes of a piano or flute, or the gap between the in-breath and the out-breath. When you pay attention to those gaps, awareness of 'something' becomes just awareness. The formless dimension of pure consciousness arises from within you and replaces identification with form."

This blank or silent gap, as Deepak Chopra points out, is the home of inner peace and enlightenment. You have a thought here, a thought here, and between every thought there's a little space.

Each time a new thought arises, as it inevitably does, don't think anything else about it, don't judge it and don't try to push it away. Instead of doing this, just "release it" and "let it go." And if you pay attention you will experience brief moments between thoughts in this space of pure awareness and silence. Initially, the experience may only last a second, or even brief microseconds, so pay close attention.

As Eckhart Tolle explains in *A New Earth*:

"You don't need to be concerned with the duration of those gaps. A few seconds is good enough. Gradually, they will lengthen themselves, without any effort on your part. More importantly than their length, is to bring them in frequently so that your daily activities and your stream of thinking become interspersed with space."

In "*The Power of Now*," Eckhart explains that "*when a thought subsides, you experience a discontinuity in the mental stream – a gap of "no-mind*." At first, the gaps will be short, a few seconds perhaps, but gradually they will become longer. When these gaps occur, you feel a certain stillness and peace inside you. This is the beginning of your natural state of felt oneness with Being, which is usually obscured by the mind. With practice, the sense of stillness and peace will deepen. In fact, there is no end to its depth. You will also feel a subtle emanation of joy arising from deep within: the joy of Being."

4:

Repeat the process several times. Concentrate on experiencing longer gaps. Don't judge your thoughts or engage in them. Just observe them, say "yes" and release them while concentrating on experiencing the gaps.

LESSON 5

THE ILLUSION OF WORDS AND THOUGHTS

"My teaching is like a finger pointing to the moon. Do not mistake the finger for the moon."

Gautama Buddha

HUMAN THINKING, AS WE KNOW, is mostly based on *"words,"* which constitute the basis or oral speech and verbal thinking.

Words, however, are only symbols. But most people seem to forget this!

The word *"moon"* for example, is used to represent the real moon. But it is not the actual moon. In fact, someone who has never seen the moon or its picture cannot *"imagine"* the real moon unless he actually sees it. In any other case, his mental representation of the moon will necessarily be inaccurate, false.

Likewise, when we speak of "Truth" or "Illusion", there is no way you can truly understand their meaning unless you actually experience them. This is why the Buddha advised his followers not to try to understand his teachings rationally, or to stick to his words, but to try to see beyond instead:

The Buddha said:

"My teaching is like a finger pointing to the moon. Do not mistake the finger for the moon."

As this simile states, *"reality"* cannot be expressed with words. Anything you believe or say about it is only *"a finger pointing to the moon."*

And since all words are mere *"fingers pointing to the moon,"* we must be careful about what we think, say and believe. Don't fall into the senseless trap of believing that your personal interpretation of reality is the absolute truth.

Don´t be a fool for the finger is not the point…: the point is the moon!

RELATIVITY OF WORDS AND THOUGHTS

In certain parts of Thailand and Africa, the natives hold peculiar beliefs and values regarding beauty. Their particular ideal of female beauty consists in elongated necks, produced by primitive neck-stretching techniques. To these girls there is only one Truth: *"The longer the better!"*

Stretching the girl´s necks is a long and harsh process…

As early as the age of two, the small girls start wearing metal rings that are gradually increased in length, and that actually stretch their necks a few inches in a matter of one or two decades. And the lifelong process never stops.

All these girls believe that the longer their necks are, the prettier they will look. They also believe that having a short neck is synonymous of *"ugliness."* So they all have one big desire:

"Having the longest or one of the longest necks!"

This real-life example depicts what I call *"the relativity of beauty."* Truth is, like the Greek philosopher Plato allegedly said:

"Beauty lies in the eyes of the beholder."

The ideal of beauty no only changes from place to place, but also from time to time. What we consider *"beautiful"* today doesn't necessarily mean it was considered *"beautiful"* in the past and vice versa.

In the early 1900's, for example, the female beauty ideal was mid-sized and a bit *"robust"* or *"chubby"* The most popular hairstyle at the time was a bob. And women *"bound their breasts"* to give themselves a more boyish figure. Back then, athletic, thin and strong females were simply not seen as *"beautiful"* or *"attractive,"* like today.

Take Mary Pickford, for example, the Canadian-American silent film actress and co-founder of the film studio United Artists. She was a very short and somewhat round-faced woman. Nevertheless, people at the time saw her as *"the most beautiful woman on earth"* and compared the shape of her face with *"the roundness of childhood."*

Pickford's famous curls, according to the press at the time, made her look *"like a living doll."* Everyone said *"the camera loved her"* and no actress before her had ever been loved more by her audience. In fact, she was considered so *"beautiful"* and *"charming,"* that she became the first movie actress known as *"America's sweetheart"* (an honor many decades later shared with Sandra Bullock, a real *"no-beauty"* according to 1900 standards).

Regarding the "relativity of beauty," the founder of Taoism, the philosopher, and poet of ancient China Lao-Tzu (6th century BC) explained that as soon as you define *"beauty"* then *"ugliness"* is automatically defined. This occurs because our mind is ruled by *"duality,"* that is, in a world of *"opposite sides,"* in which everything is valued regarding *"good"* and *"bad."*

Let´s take a glance at what Lao-Tzu wrote over two thousand years ago in his celebrated masterpiece the *Tao Te King*:

> *"When people see some things as beautiful, other things become ugly. When people see some things as good, other things become bad... Under heaven, all can see beauty as beauty only because there is ugliness. All can know good as good only because there is evil."*

To this, the celebrated Taoist master Chuang Tzu (4th century BC) added the following:

> *"Everyone has his own conception of beauty and therefore establishes ugliness. Everyone has his own conception of Goodness and therefore establishes evil".*

In any case, our individual appreciation of beauty and goodness will always depend on our personal beliefs, values, and desires.

And, as we will see in this chapter, these are initially set in our early childhood and unconsciously and define our present personality and behavior.

ADOPTING BELIEFS, VALUES AND DESIRES

Let's see how the interdependence between our beliefs, values, and desires sets its roots in the mind of every child through a three-stage process:

1: Establishing a set of beliefs: As a child, you receive a "set of beliefs" from your parents, relatives, teachers, friends and social environment, among others. These beliefs depend on your "mental chatter" to grow and become stronger. The more you think about them positively, the stronger they will get.

For example:

"Long necks make women beautiful."

2: Establishing a scale of values: Based on those beliefs, as a child you unconsciously establish a "basic list or scale" of things that you believe are "good" and of thing that you believe are "bad." As a child, you will naturally "value" the "good things" more than the "bad things". And the more you think about the things you most value, the stronger your scale of values will be.

For example:

"Women with long necks are better and more valuable whereas those with short necks are worse and less valuable."

3: Establishment of personal desires: Finally, the more you "value" something, the more you will cherish or desire it. And the less you "value" it, the less you will want it. Also, "better" and "more valuable" things will always make you feel "good" and not having them will always you feel "bad."

It's plain to see that your personal desires depend on your personal set of values, and that these, in turn, depend on your personal set of beliefs.

For example:

If you accept that women with long necks are "better" or "prettier" than those with short ones, then you will undoubtedly experience one of these two desires:

1: *If I am a female, I will naturally desire a long neck.*

2: *If I am a male, I will naturally desire a woman with a long neck.*

And thus the personal desire for long necks is born!

THE NATURE OF ABSTRACT CONCEPTS

One of the most unwanted consequences of the prehistoric birth of human language together with what Eckhart calls our *"incessant stream of thinking"* is that our remote ancestors began thinking about everything and at all times, creating new words to describe all sorts of *"abstract concepts"* and *"speculations."*

These include imaginary and abstract concepts such as justice, happiness, freedom, worthiness, beauty, glory, courage, goodness, realization, duty, merit, power, manners, legal, success, and honor, among others.

Of course, these concepts differ from person to person, from place to place, and from time to time. And despite the fact that they are abstract and therefore non-existent, they affect our lives in the form of different beliefs, values, and desires.

One of the abstract terms that have caused more problems is the concept of time, a direct consequence of the *"invention"* of the abstract words: *"past,"* *"present"* and *"future."*

Among the most critical abstract beliefs adopted by humans stand good and evil, better and worse, success and failure and happiness and unhappiness, just to name a few.

THE ILLUSORY NATURE OF OUR BELIEFS

As we have seen, ever since you were a child, you have been collecting an uncountable number of *"accepted beliefs."*

These include many cultural, religious, political and social beliefs that you initially *"learned"* from your parents, grandparents, and teachers, as well as from countless sources during your growing years and adulthood.

As you grow older, some beliefs may pass from being perceived as "*good*" and "*desired*," to "*bad*" and "*unwanted*," while others may turn out being wrong, as for example the ancient belief that the world is flat.

Since it looked flat, people thought it was actually flat. And for thousands of years that became the "*generally accepted truth*" - but only until science proved them wrong.

Human history is full of examples of other "*accepted truths*" that were once widely accepted and that as time passed turned out to be "*false beliefs*" and even "*incoherent*" and "*absurd*."

Here are some examples of "*false beliefs*" that were once considered absolute truths. And the astounding list continues to grow:

The notion that our planet occupies the very center of the universe and that the sun, moon, stars, and planets all revolve around us. (Geocentric astronomic theory).

The theory that states that all human thinking takes place in the stomach (Aristotelian anatomy).

The notion that the world is flat and that if you sail far enough from the coast you will inevitably fall off its edge and perish (Medieval astronomy and navigation)

The scientific theory that establishes that space and time truly exist and that they are absolute (Pre-Einstein mechanic physics).

The belief in supernatural beings, dragons, ogres, gnomes, leprechauns, trolls, fairies, unicorns, centaurs, genies, werewolves, vampires, zombies, witches, trolls, and other imaginary creatures (Olden folk tales).

The conviction that we control our minds instead of our unconscious (Pre-Freudian psychology)

The practice of massively sacrificing humans as the most effective way to please the gods and obtain their favors, especially young virgins (Aztec religion).

The notion that if God had wanted man to fly he would have given him wings (Popular saying before the invention of the airplane)

91

The legal permission to capture, buy and sell Afro-Americans and enslave them (USA before the Abolition of slavery)

The social norm that established that gentlemen in full dress should wear wigs, diligently powdered to give a distinctive white or off-white color (18th Century English etiquette)

The claim that Germany's Aryan race is "the world's superior race" and therefore must rule over the other races (Nazi philosophy).

And the list goes on and on...

These beliefs were doomed to perish. Surprisingly, they were considered undisputed truths by millions of people before being trashed.

So, what makes you sure that your present beliefs are really true?

How many "common beliefs" are wrong without you or anyone else knowing about it?

Is there any guarantee that any of them are true?

The following principle answers the question:

If a belief is based on abstract concepts, then it does not have a real essence and, wrong or right, it is only an illusion.

THE ILLUSORY SCALE OF VALUES

As I explained earlier, based on our particular beliefs, everyone creates a personal scale of values by which "we measure all things." However, these values are basically subjective. That is, they depend on *"the eye of the beholder"* and are therefore unreal.

One way of evidencing that our present values are not absolute and are therefore unreal, is that your complete set of values is not the same as mine or anyone else's.

We all have different values because we all have different beliefs.

For example, the values of a samurai warrior are not the same as those of a Wall Street broker.

The values of the Dalai Lama are different from those of a Mafia hit-man.

And the values of an Australian aborigine has almost nothing to do with those of a Russian astronaut.

In all cases, our values determine our behavior. And, as history and experience evidence, what's good for one person is often bad for another.

In Cambodia, for example, it is considered "an honor" to eat one of their most popular national dishes. Would you like to try it? With so little information, you probably don't know what to say. Let me give you a clue:

The Cambodian dish is often described as "crispy on the outside, with tender white meat inside and a vague taste of chicken or cod."

You probably still don't know if you'd like to try it or not. Why? Because you still don't know what it is and therefore don't know what to believe. However, if you like meat and crispy food, perhaps you would end up trying it. I know I wouldn't. Why? Because the popular Cambodian dish I'm talking about is *tarantula spiders in dipping sauce!*

You may feel repulse, indifference or your mouth may water. It all depends on your personal set of beliefs and values. If you were Cambodian, as well as your parents, you probably would have eaten a few tarantulas.

Based on all the above, and applying Albert Einstein's Theory of Relativity, we can formulate the following principle:

All our beliefs, values and desires are relative and therefore unreal for they vary from person to person and depend on relative and erroneous perceptions and points of views.

ILLUSORY CRAVINGS AND DESIRES

Just as our beliefs give birth to our scale of values, with which we *"measure all things,"* our scale of values gives birth to our cravings and desires.

According to the teachings of the Buddha, *"pain or suffering arises through desire or craving."* And desires and cravings, according to what we have seen, arise from the endless *"chatter in our minds."*

Hinduism teaches us that unfulfilled desires cause suffering and that the more desires we wish to fulfill, the more we suffer while they remain unfulfilled. Therefore, freedom from desires always leads to freedom from suffering.

This is why Buddha said that *"to be free of pain we need to cut the bonds of desire."*

However, being free from desire doesn't imply having no desires at all. We can be free and still have healthy desires, like reading this book, for instance, or wanting to go out for dinner tonight, as long as we don't allow ourselves to be bound to our desires. See the difference?

The secret to overcoming desire is not to lose all our desires, but to transform all our binding desires into non-binding ones. And you can only achieve this by draining the power from your ego and taking the reins of your life in your own hands.

"Be Present. Be there as the observer of the mind. Instead of quoting the Buddha, be the Buddha, be '*the awakened one*,' which is what the word Buddha truly means."

* * *

DO NOT BELIEVE
Buddha

"Do not believe in anything
simply because you have heard it.
Do not believe in anything
simply because it is spoken
and rumoured by many.

Do not believe in anything
simply because it is found
written in your religious books.

97

Do not believe in anything
merely on the authority of
your teachers and elders.

Do not believe in traditions
because they have been
handed down for many generations.

But after observation and analysis,
when you find that anything
agrees with reason and is
conducive to the good and
benefit of one and all,
then accept it and live up to it."

(The Anguttara Nikaya)

* * *

FIFTH EXERCISE

EXPERIENCING YOUR INNER BODY

"Direct your attention into the body. Feel it from within. Is it alive? Is there life in your hands, arms, legs, and feet - in your abdomen, your chest? Can you feel the subtle energy field that pervades the entire body and gives vibrant life to every organ and every cell? Can you feel it simultaneously in all parts of the body as a single field of energy? Keep focusing on the feeling of your inner body for a few moments. Do not start to think about it. Feel it. The more attention you give it, the clearer and stronger this feeling will become."

Eckhart Tolle

ECKHART   TOLLE   RECOMMENDS "experiencing presence" as one way of slowing down your thoughts and begin to stop the never-ending "*mental chatter*." And that's the basis of this exercise.

According to Eckhart, to experience presence, you must keep in mind the following two basic principles:

> *The body is "the vehicle for experiencing presence."*

> **"You cannot experience presence in your mind."*

The following exercise is one way of experiencing presence. Just follow these steps:

1: Close your eyes and concentrate on "feeling" your hands. Try to feel a "tingling" or "warmth" within them. You can do it if you concentrate enough. You will soon feel it. Eckhart calls this tingling or warmth "your inner sense of aliveness."

It is your inner presence and being-ness, the *'you'* that you really are, that is, your natural, inner consciousness or Self. Concentrate. Feel it. Experience it.

2: Once you have experienced the "tingling" or "warmth" in your hands, then proceed to observe your thoughts, as you did in the previous exercises. Close your eyes. No matter what you're thinking, realize that you are having a thought and identify it. Once you recognize it, say "yes" out loud and, without engaging in your first thought, leave it for later and let it go as before.

3: As soon as you release your last thought, take your attention away from thinking and concentrate on your hands. Feel the warmth or the inner tingling of its energy (its "aliveness"). Concentrate on this feeling and also experience the "gap."

This will undoubtedly help you help you slow down your thoughts. Although Eckhart recommends focusing on the hands, it doesn't matter what part of your body you focus on. What's important is that you take your focus **away** from your thoughts and focus on something physical.

By taking your focus and attention away from your thoughts and placing it on something physical (and therefore more "real") you will be able to slow down your mind and silence your thoughts, allowing you to experience the "gaps."

4: Try to keep mental silence. Be the Observer, that is, your Self. Sooner or later "the voice inside your head" will throw in a new thought. Recognize it as something different that your Self. Recognize it as your "ego." And as soon as you have an idea, recognize it, say "yes" and let it go, before concentrating once more on the tingling or warmth of your hands.

5: Do this with different parts of your body until you manage to experience your complete inner body as a whole. Try to feel the subtle energy field that fills your entire body and gives vibrant life to every organ and every cell and also try to feel it simultaneously in all parts of the body as a single field of energy. As you concentrate on what you feel, keep your mind blank and continue observing your thoughts. Every time a new thought arrives, observe it, recognize it and let it go - leave it for later. Then immediately concentrate on the tingling of your inner body and experience the "gap."

6: Repeat this process several times (for one or two minutes) and try to do this exercise several times a day. It will allow you to get in touch with what Eckhart calls "your inner sense of aliveness." This, as he says, is the subtle sense of aliveness. And concentrating on it is an excellent way of bringing your awareness to the present moment.

LESSON 6

THE ILLUSION OF TIME

"The secret of health for both mind and body is not to mourn for the past, nor to worry about the future, but to live the present moment wisely and earnestly."

Gautama Buddha

ACCORDING TO ALBERT EINSTEIN, *"time is an illusion."* In fact, his famous Theory of Relativity proved that "time is always relative" and that "absolute time" does not exist. In other words, that what we call time is really "our own relative perception" and is therefore only "an illusion."

It took Einstein years of hard work to reach this conclusion. Before his work, scientists believed time was absolute and that it elapsed with the same speed here, there and everywhere in the universe. But he proved them wrong!

Sixteen years after Einstein's death, a group of scientists conducted a series of experiments to determine if he was right or not regarding the relativity of time and that absolute time didn't exist. Back then many distinguished scientists still believed it did and that what Einstein claimed was impossible!

One of the most polemical principles they publicly rejected was that, according to Einstein, '*the faster you go, the slower time passes.*'

This was utter madness; they cried out: "Time is a universal phenomenon, Einstein is wrong! Time passes at the same speed everywhere! Always at the same velocity, both here and in the furthest corner of creation! If this were not so, the whole universe would not exist!"

THE TIME DILATION EXPERIMENTS

In October 1971, a group of scientists led by Joseph C. Hafele, a physicist, and Richard E. Keating set out to prove that Einstein was right. Their work is known as the "time dilation experiments."

First, Hafele and Keating got hold of three macroscopic clocks, that is, cesium atomic beam clocks capable of measuring down to one nanosecond, which is one billionth of a second.

Second, they needed to find two turbojets capable of flying at high speed. They wanted to leave one of the macroscopic clocks on land and fly the other two at high speed to see if there was the most minimal change.

If Einstein was right, there should be a slight difference between the clock left on land and the other two, which would allegedly "tick" slower.

The best solution they could find was flying them on commercial jet flights around the world twice, once eastward and once westward. And that's what they did.

According to the U.S. Naval Observatory, the flying clocks lost 59+/-10 nanoseconds during the eastward trip and gained 273+/-7 nanosecond during the westward trip. This proved that, effectively, time is not an absolute value but a relative one and therefore has no real essence.

Like Einstein said, *"time is an illusion"*!

THE THREE TENSES OF TIME

Back in the Stone Age, the abstract concept of time shook humankind. A mere invention it was. But it still has not ceased to stir us all!

Never before had such a tremendous power been released by a single word.

Based on primitive logic, the concept of time was developed based on three other abstract concepts that shook the world:

1: Now

2: Before

3: After

Later known as:

1: Present.

2: Past

3: Future

Just like the apparent movement of the sun across the sky and the apparent flatness of the earth, the apparent march of time also fooled our ancestors when they began to create abstract concepts and beliefs based on their own reasoning.

If we examine each one of time's three tenses we will find the following:

1: The future has not taken place. So it still does not exist.

2: The past already took place. So it ceased to exist.

3: And the present passes by so fast that by the time you say "this is the present" it's not the present instant anymore!

These three tenses are the basis of what is known as "psychological time" which only exists in our minds.

THE NOW IS EVER PRESENT

Apart from psychological time, there exists the ever-present Now, as Krishnamurti explains in his *Collected Works (Vol. IV,12):*

> *"The present is the eternal. Through time, the timeless is not experienced. 'The now' is ever existent; even if you escape into future, 'the now' is ever present. The present is the doorway to the past.*
>
> *"If you do not understand the present now, will you understand it in the future? What you are now you will be, if the present is not understood.   Understanding   comes   only*

through the present: postponement does not yield comprehension.

"Time is transcended only in the stillness of the present. This tranquility is not to be gained through time, through 'becoming' tranquil; there must be stillness, not the becoming still. We look at time as a means to become. This becoming is endless: it is not the eternal, the timeless. The becoming is endless conflict, leading to illusion. In the stillness of the present is the eternal.

"The now is ever existent; even if you escape into future, the now is ever present through becoming tranquil..."

BREAK FREE FROM PSYCHOLOGICAL TIME

When we speak of being in the present moment, we are not talking about the psychological present. Why? Because there is a clear distinction between psychological time and what we call "chronological time."

Psychological time, as Eckhart Tolle explains, *"is identification with the past and continuous compulsive projection into the future... The enlightened people's main focus of attention is always the Now, but they are still peripherally aware of time. In other words, they continue to use clock time but are free of psychological time."*

According to him, psychological time has generated a mental disease in humans, who believe they can build a better future and that the end justifies the means. This is why most humans are always trying to get somewhere other than where they are and basing their lives on finding a means to this end.

They are not satisfied with their present lives. They imagine a better future, a better "them," and experience life as if their happiness is always waiting just around the corner.   And nevertheless, no matter how much they try, they are never able to find nor grasp it truly.

JESUS AND LIVING IN THE NOW

Jesus highlighted the importance of not being trapped in psychological time in his celebrated Sermon of the Mount, in which he said, as Mathew 6 states:

> *"You are the salt of the earth; but if the salt loses its flavor, how shall it be seasoned? It is then good for nothing but to be thrown out and trampled underfoot by men.*

> *"You are the light of the world. A city that is set on a hill cannot be hidden. Nor do they light a lamp and put it under a basket, but on*

a lampstand, and it gives light to all who are in the house.

"Let your light so shine before men, that they may see your good works and glorify your Father in heaven.

Let go of your past

"You have heard that it was said to those of old, 'You shall not murder, and whoever murders will be in danger of the judgment.' But I say, even if you are angry with someone, you are subject to judgment! And whoever says to his brother, 'Idiot!' shall be in danger of the court. But whoever curses someone shall be in danger of the fires of hell.

"Therefore if you bring your gift to the altar, and there remember that your brother has something against you, leave your gift there before the altar, and go your way.

"First be reconciled to your brother, and then come and offer your gift. Agree with your adversary quickly, while you are on the way with him, lest your adversary deliver you

to the judge, the judge hand you over to the officer, and you be thrown into prison.

"Assuredly, I say to you, you will by no means get out of there till you have paid the last penny.

Don't worry about the future

"Therefore I say to you, do not worry about your life, what you will eat or what you will drink; nor about your body, what you will put on.

"Is not life more than food and the body more than clothing?

"Look at the birds of the air, for they neither sow nor reap nor gather into barns; yet your heavenly Father feeds them.

"Are you not of more value than they?

"Which of you by worrying can add one cubit to his stature?

"So why do you worry about clothing?

"Consider the lilies of the field, how they grow: they neither toil nor spin; and yet I say to you that even Solomon in all his glory was not arrayed like one of these.

"Now if God so clothes the grass of the field, which today is, and tomorrow is thrown into the oven, will He not much more clothe you, O you of little faith?

"Therefore do not worry, saying: 'What shall we eat?' or 'What shall we drink?' or 'What shall we wear?' For after all these things the Gentiles seek. For your heavenly Father knows that you need all these things. But seek first the kingdom of God and His righteousness, and all these things shall be added to you.

"Therefore do not worry about tomorrow, for tomorrow will worry about its own things. Enough for each day is its own trouble."

AN OPTICAL DELUSION OF CONSCIOUSNESS
Albert Einstein

A human being is part of the whole so-called universe... We experience ourselves, our thoughts and feelings as something separate from the rest (from the universe). A kind of optical delusion of consciousness!

This delusion is a kind of prison for us, restricting us to our personal desires and to affection for a few persons nearest to us.

Our task must be to free ourselves from the prison by widening our circle of compassion to embrace all living creatures and the whole of nature in its beauty (the whole universe).

The true value of a human being is determined by the measure and the sense in which they have obtained liberation from the self. We shall require a substantially new manner of thinking if humanity is to survive.

A. J. P A R R

SIXTH EXERCISE

BREATHING MEDITATION

"Conscious breathing, which is a powerful meditation in its own right, will gradually put you in touch with the body. Follow the breath with your attention as it moves in and out of your body. Breathe into the body, and feel your abdomen expanding and contracting slightly with each inhalation and exhalation..."

Eckhart Tolle

ACCORDING TO ANCIENT BUDDHISTS, Gautama Buddha was only a small child when a remarkable incident took place: The boy "spontaneously discovered" the technique of "breathing meditation," and suffered a surprising spiritual trance that, later, during his search for truth in early adulthood, was key to his enlightenment.

It all began when his parents took him to the annual Indian celebration called the Plowing Festival, a popular feast to promote agriculture. It was a happy occasion for both nobles and commoners.

When the ceremony began, his parents left the young boy on a screened and canopied couch under the cool shade of a rose-apple tree. There he was to be watched by several maids in charge of his care. But when the festival was at its height, the maids went off to watch the ceremony and left the young boy alone.

After they left to see the spectacle, the boy found himself alone and in complete calm under the rose-apple tree. Sitting with his back straight on the canopied couch and with his legs crossed, he closed his eyes and started to play a game: He listened to the sounds that surrounded him, the chirping of the birds and the blowing of the wind. As he played with his eyes closed, he carefully listened to every sound, every noise that surrounded him. But what started out as innocent entertainment suddenly took a twist when his "listening game" switched from the outer sounds of nature to the inner sound of his breath.

Concentrating on his breath, his "inner chatter" diminished and ceased.

The young boy went into a trance!

And thus, Gautama spontaneously "discovered" the science of breath meditation.

According to the ancient scriptures, "all the conditions conducive to quiet meditation were there. So, the pensive child, young in years but old in wisdom, sat cross-legged and seized the opportunity to commence that all-important practice of intense concentration on the breath. His exhalations and inhalations thus gained for him the 'one-pointedness of mind' known as Samadhi (Oneness or mindfulness), and he experienced the first jhāna (ecstasy)."

Once the festival ended, the maids as well as the boy's parents returned and found the young prince sitting cross-legged, plunged in deep meditation.

Many years later, when seeking realization, Gautama left his home and spent six years with a group of ascetic monks or "sadhus," who practiced the Hindu way of renunciation or "sannyasa." Hoping to find enlightenment, he lived like a mendicant (beggar) and encouraged abstinence and self-mortification. However, as time passed, he realized the futility of his efforts.

Disillusioned and invaded with deep sorrow, one morning he left the ascetics and continued his search for spiritual realization on his own. And it is said that shortly after he was resting under a Bodhi tree when he remembered his experience at the Plowing Festival, when he was only a child. And thus he discovered what is presently known as the cornerstone of Buddhist meditation, which led him to Nirvana or enlightenment.

BREATHING MEDITATION EXERCISE

I learned this basic meditation technique when I was seventeen. It´s very simple. To practice it, just follow these steps:

1: Sit or lie down in a comfortable and relaxing position. The position you now have while reading this book will do. You can also adopt another one or maybe a meditation or yoga pose.

2: Close your eyes and listen to the sound of your breath. That will be your "mantra" or "sacred word." Listen to your breath. Don´t control it, just listen and be the Observer.

3: If a thought arises, observe it, understand it and let it go. Try to feel the "gaps" between each thought.

4: To slow down your thoughts, listen to the sound of your breath and also "feel" the movement of your lungs, the movement of your chest and abdomen slowly expanding and contracting as the air moves in and out… Don´t try to control your breath. Let it go. Be the Observer. Concentrate. Feel it. Experience it. "One conscious breath is enough to make some space where before there was the uninterrupted succession of one thought after another."

5: Repeat the process as each new thought arises. Don´t reject them. Observe them, let them go and concentrate on your breath. Realize that breathing isn't something you do but something you witness or observe. Breathing is autonomous and effortless. Your unconscious inner intelligence is in charge of it. Just be the Observer. Just be the Witness. If you slow down your "inner chat" and experience the gaps between thoughts, you won't lose yourself in your thoughts and will experience the Now.

6: Repeat this exercise as often as you can. Combine them with the others. Work on one a few days and then on another, until you find the one that best suits you according to your capacity and level of practice.

LEVEL THREE

THE MASTER

Mastering the Art of Being Present

With due knowledge and sufficient practice always comes Mastery. Once the practitioner masters the ancient art of Being Present in the Now, the inner Self or Being gradually surges from within and can be personally felt —though never understood intellectually. When practicing the Art of Being Present, advanced practitioners may experience occasional "altered states of consciousness" as well as "non-dual states of consciousness." Known in Hinduism as "Savikalpa Samadhi," these altered states of consciousness are often described as states of "Beingness," that is, of "being aware of one's existence without thinking," characterized by bliss (ananda) and joy (sukha). This process implies regaining awareness of our inner Being and being continuously Present in the Now, enjoying an internalized state of awareness and inner peace often described as "awakened consciousness" or "enlightenment."

LESSON 7

A TRIP BACK HOME

"Many who seek quietness of mind withdraw from active life to a village, to a monastery, to the mountains, or they withdraw into ideas, enclose themselves in a belief or avoid people who give them trouble. Such isolation is not stillness of mind. The enclosure of the mind in an idea or the avoidance of people who make life complicated does not bring about stillness of mind. Stillness of mind comes only when there is no process of isolation through accumulation but a complete understanding of the whole process of relationship...

"*In that stillness, there is no formulation; there is no idea, there is no memory; that stillness is a state of creation that can be experienced only when there is a complete understanding of the whole process of the `me.' Otherwise, stillness has no meaning. Only in that stillness, which is not a result, is the eternal discovered, which is beyond time.*"

Krishnamurti

IF YOU MANAGED TO REACH THIS LESSON, I assume that you have practiced all the previous exercises presented in this workbook. These, together with the theory contained in each lesson, are basically all you will need to get started.

Remember that according to Eckhart, the number and duration of the gaps between thoughts will increase with practice and will get more intense.

One more thing: If you are looking for spiritual progress, don't expect to find "rational" or "logical" answers to all your questions. Spiritual growth doesn't depend on intellectual knowledge.

Like the Buddha once said:

> *"Suppose a man is struck by a poisoned arrow and the doctor wishes to take out the arrow immediately. Suppose the man does not want the arrow removed until he knows who shot it, his age, his parents, and why he shot it. What would happen? If he were to wait until all these questions have been answered, the man might die first."*

MEISTER ECKHART AND LIVING IN THE NOW

Remember to live in the Now, keeping in mind what seven centuries ago the Dominican monk known as Meister Eckhart expressed:

"Nothing in all creation is so like God as stillness."

"Time is what keeps the light from reaching us. There is no greater obstacle to God than time: and not only time but temporalities, not only temporal things but temporal affections, not only temporal affections but the very taint and smell of time…"

"Spirituality is not to be learned by flight from the world, or by running away from things, or by turning solitary and going apart from the world. Rather, we must learn an inner solitude wherever or with whomsoever we may be. We must learn to penetrate things and find God there (and Now)…"

FINAL FREEDOM FROM MENTAL SLAVERY

If you identify yourself with your *"chattering mind,"* you will become a *"slave"* of your own mind. Like Ramana Maharshi said: *"The mind is Maya."* So use Maya to free yourself from illusion. *The* only way to realize that you are truly a slave of your mind and that you must free yourself from its influence is by following the ancient maxim inscribed in the Temple of Apollo at Delphi: *"Know thyself."*

That's basically it: *You need Self-knowledge. You need to observe your mind. You need to experience inner stillness. You need to "live in the Now."* If not, then you will forever sink in the quicksand of delusion, experiencing unhappiness, sadness, fear, rage, and powerlessness, doomed to *"see only what the veil of Maya wants you to see."*

Removing the veil of Maya and seeing what lies behind it takes knowledge, practice, strength, and courage. Hindu sages and gurus often compare it with taking "a trip back home." And so, my fellow reader, as our planet spins and travels, as the stars continue shining, profoundly sink in the "present moment" and you'll be on your way back home...

NAMASTE!

* * *

<u>THE AWAKENED ONE</u>

Do not seek outside your head.

Observe your mind.

Don't think about doing "this" or "that."

Simply become present.

Do it now.

Be the "Observer of the mind."

Be the Buddha.

Be "The Awakened One"

* * *

SEVENTH EXERCISE

THE AWAKENING TECHNIQUE

"Transformation is not in the future, can never be in the future. It can only be now, from moment to moment. So what do we mean by transformation? Surely it is very simple: seeing the false as the false and the true as the true. Seeing the truth in the false and seeing the false in that which has been accepted as the truth. Seeing the false as the false and the true as the true is transformation, because when you see something very clearly as the truth, that truth liberates. When you see that something is false, that false thing drops away.

"When you see that ceremonies are mere vain repetitions, when you see the truth of it and do not justify it, there is transformation, is there not? Because another bondage is gone. When you see that class distinction is false, that it creates conflict, creates misery, division between people - when you see the truth of it, that very truth liberates. The very perception of that truth is transformation, is it not?

"As we are surrounded by so much that is false, perceiving the falseness from moment to moment is transformation. Truth is not cumulative. It is from moment to moment. That which is cumulative, accumulated, is a memory, and through memory, you can never find the truth, for memory depends on time - time being the past, the present and the future. Time, which is continuity, can never find that which is eternal; eternity is not continuity. That which endures is not eternal. Eternity is in the moment. Eternity is in the now. The now is not the reflection of the past nor the continuance of the past through the present to the future."

Krishnamurti

THE AWAKENING TECHNIQUE IS a powerful *mini-meditation* that allows us to temporarily interrupt our "mental chatter" at will, that is, anytime and anywhere we want or need to!

Once you learn this technique, it will be relatively easy for you to apply it whenever you wish! I use it almost every day. More than a technique for reaching enlightenment, it is a powerful way to stop our "mental chatter" (at least temporarily) allowing us to briefly experience inner stillness and peace.

I recommend it in case of emergencies, when we are facing a stressful situation, and we urgently need to stop our own "mental chatter" and take a break from excessive thinking! We can stop our monologue, at least for a few minutes, while we relax and "recharge batteries." And we can also use this technique to "boost" your concentration when practicing "mantra meditation" or "breath meditation."

A BREAKTHROUGH TECHNIQUE

The Awakening Technique can help you by slowing down and even disappearing your "inner chat" when you most need to. It will also allow you to "recharge" yourself by giving yourself a break and not thinking for a few minutes.

I have found that it is the ideal practical and immediate solution when you find yourself:

*Excessively "tied up" in your thoughts and can't stop thinking.

*Excessively disappointed with something, someone or yourself.

*Excessively worried about someone, something or yourself.

*Excessively angry at someone, something or yourself.

*Excessively sad about someone, something or yourself.

*Excessively excited about something, someone, or yourself.

*Excessively confused about someone, something, or yourself.

*Excessively afraid of someone or something.

*Excessively insomniac.

*Excessively discouraged.

*Excessively depressed.

*Excessively nervous.

In sum, The Awakening Technique can actually help you *ANY TIME YOU NEED TO STOP YOUR INNER CHAT!*

THE TECHNIQUE´S BASIC STEPS.

1: Sit or lie down in a comfortable and relaxing position. The position you now have while reading this book will do. You can also adopt another one or maybe a meditation or yoga pose.

2: Close your eyes. Listen to your breath or mentally repeat the universal mantra Om, whichever suits you best. Whatever you choose, that "sound" or "mantra" will be your "Stimulus Number One." Remember that.

3: Listen to your mantra (breath or Om) and as soon as a new thought arrives you know what to do: observe it, understand it, let it go and get back to repeating the mantra. But this time we will add a second stimulus.

4: As you continue "listening" to your mantra (breath or Om) gently touch the tips of your thumbs with the tips of your index fingers and gently rub them, with minimal movements, minimal frictions, minimal rubs. This sensation or feeling will be your "Stimulus Number Two." Remember that.

5: Concentrate on the sound of your mantra (breath or Om) and at the same time feel the tip of your fingers rubbing. This double-feeling will help you slow down your thoughts. Nevertheless, a new thought is bound to appear. When it does, recognize it, let it go and get back to feeling the mantra (breath or Om) and the sensation of your fingers rubbing. And now you are ready to add your third and last stimulus.

6: You will really need to concentrate on doing this step. But once you master it you will find that it is really quite simple. And, as you will see, it has countless applications.

Concentrate. Listen to your mantra (breath or Om) and at the same time concentrate on the feeling of your fingers rubbing.

Try to feel both stimuli at the same time, can you?

If not, please return to the last step and repeat it until you succeed. It's not that hard. A bit of practice will do.

If you do manage to perceive the sound of the mantra and the touch of your fingers at the same time, you're ready to add the third and last stimulus that will stop your "inner chat":

7: Don't stop concentrating on the first two stimuli (mantra and fingers) and only add the third stimulus:

Listen to all the sounds that surround you.

7. Concentrate on the three stimuli at the same time. It takes so much concentration that you will virtually have no space for thinking. If you have a thought, it's only because you stopped concentrating on one of the three stimuli, maybe two or even all. If you do, I figure by now you know what to do: Observe your thought, understand what it's about, leave it for later, let it go and continue concentrating on your three stimuli at the same time:

*Your sacred mantra (Internal Sound).

*Your sense of touch (Fingers Rubbing)

*Your sense of hearing (External Sound).

8: Practice this exercise at least twice a day. If you manage to experience the three stimuli at the same time, you will certainly experience brief gaps of non-thinking almost immediately (guaranteed). This is simple because our conscious minds find it hard to consciously pay complete attention to three things at the same time. So taking advantage of this "disadvantage," we can defeat our wandering and ever-chattering mind, forcing it to shut up at least for short periods of time or "gaps" that become longer with practice, as Eckhart Tolle and Deepak Chopra claim. And these "gaps," as they explain, are the gateway for living in the Now and for definitely entering the Path of Self-Realization and Enlightenment.

OTHER COMBINATIONS:

Remember, this technique works by combining three different stimuli, like for example listening to the sounds around you, feeling something with your fingers and chewing gum. As long as there are at least three, it will work.

Here are other possible stimuli you can use (combine 3):

Feel the tingling of your hands.

Feel the tingling of your whole body.

Gently rub, caress or scratch any part of your body.

Press or rub your tongue against your lower teeth.

Hold your hands together and feel their contact.

Hold your hands in praying position and feel their touch.

Smell a penetrating fragrance like aromatic incense.

Play some spiritual or meditation music.

Pinch yourself anywhere you like.

Feel the water as you take a shower or bath.

Eat and slowly taste delicious food.

Enjoy sexual intercourse without saying a word.

EVERYDAY USE OF THE TECHNIQUE:

I use The Awakening Technique almost every day. Especially when I'm walking around, or waiting in line for a while.

No matter where you are or what you are doing you can use The Awakening Technique to "anchor" yourself in the present moment and stop your "inner conversation with yourself." Here's what you need to do:

1: If you are walking, for example, or driving or standing in line, gently rub the tip of your thumb and index finger and concentrate on feeling this sensation (We will call it Stimulus One). If you're driving, you can gently rub the steering wheel with minimal movements if you like, making it imperceptible to anyone who sees you doing it.

2: As you rub your fingertips, press or rub the tip off your tongue against your lower teeth. Feel this and also feel the tips of your fingers rubbing. Rubbing your teeth with the tip of your tongue will also be imperceptible to anyone who sees you or who you're driving with. One you feel both stimuli at the same time you are ready for the final step.

3: As you continue feeling the touch of your finger or fingers, together with the sensation of your tongue rubbing against your teeth add the third and final stimulus:

Listen to all the sounds that surround you.

It can be the birds chirping or whatever's on the radio or TV. Or maybe some dogs barking or vehicles passing by. Whatever you hear will do. It can be children playing, cars honking, cows mooing, or your favorite music playing. It can be whatever you hear at that moment, as long that it is a real external sound. That will do.

As you listen to all the sounds that surround you, continue feeling the touch of your finger or fingers, together with the sensation of your tongue rubbing against your teeth.

4. Concentrate on the three stimuli at the same time. It will take so much concentration that you won't have space for thinking. If you do have a thought, it's only because you stopped perceiving one of the three stimuli, or maybe two or even all. And if this

happens, you know what to do: Observe your thought, understand what it´s about, leave it for later, let it go and continue concentrating on your three stimuli.

WHEN CAN YOU USE THIS TECHNIQUE?

The Awakening Technique basically "keeps you awake," that is, it instantaneously and effectively diminishes your normal train of thoughts and allows you to "be present." Where can you use it? Anywhere!

I usually use it when:

*Walking

*Driving

*Going up or down the stairs.

*In the elevator.

*In the bus, subway or cab.

*Waiting in line.

*Waiting for someone or something.

*Taking a break from work without leaving your desk.

*Eating.

*Taking a bath.

Going to the bathroom.

Having sex.

You can practice it basically anytime and anywhere!

Do it now! Slow down your "inner chat," start to experience the "gaps" of inner stillness described by Eckhart Tolle and start experiencing the Power of Now!

A. J.   P A R R

WORKBOOK 2

FOREWORD

FACING NEGATIVITY

"Whether we are happy in our individual or family life is, in a large part, up to us. Of course, material conditions are an important factor for happiness and a good life, but one's mental attitude is of equal or greater importance."

Dalai Lama

SCIENTISTS ESTIMATE THAT IN normal conditions a human being regularly has an average of 30,000 to 40,000 daily thoughts. This means that if most of our thoughts are pessimistic, we can actually end up having tens of thousands negative thoughts in just a single day!

According to research, *"depression is always preceded by repetitive negative thinking"* and not vice versa, and *"reducing the number of negative thoughts per day actually reduces both the frequency and intensity of depressive feelings and emotions!"*

These crucial findings constitute the starting point of the 7 Lessons and 7 Exercises contained in this beginner's guidebook, which is designed to help you break the habit of negative thinking by applying the teachings of Eckhart Tolle, who claims that:

> **Most people ignore they are unceasingly generating negative thoughts and that they have the power to stop!*

> **Most people do not realize that their depression, despair, rage, hopelessness and unhappiness are generated by their own repetitive negative-thinking.*

Most people believe that in order to stop their endless flow of pessimistic thoughts they first need to get rid of their negative feelings and emotions – but it is actually the other way around!

BREAKING OUR CHILDHOOD PATTERNS

According to research, we picked up most of the thinking patterns we repeat in the present back when we were only small children and didn't know better. Fact is, each time we felt threatened, abandoned, hurt or under attack as kids, we always *"reacted defensively"* by repeating the same specific patterns of thought and behavior– such as crying, fleeing, screaming, feeling guilty, hating, cursing, fearing, attacking, blaming others or yourself, or simply ignoring the world and sinking into our own thoughts!

Studies prove that the more a child repeats frequent negative thoughts like *"no one likes me," "I hate my family," "my parents don't love me," "I feel sad,"* or *"I'm an idiot,"* the unhappier he will feel and the longer it will affect him – even during the rest of his life!

They have also found that the child will develop an increasing number of "dysfunctional" patterns, sinking deeper and deeper into a sea of suffering and experiencing life-long consequences that lead to chronic depression, illness and, in some cases, even suicide!

Let´s take a quick look, for example, at the celebrated case of 10-year-old Ulrich, who despite his young age, publicly admitted having had repetitive suicidal thoughts for years.

Ulrich was born into a dysfunctional family and admitted having a "miserable" childhood. He didn´t like school because he had a hard time socializing and *the environment was so hostile.* And he didn´t like his home either because his parents were always screaming, fighting and on the verge of divorce…

REPETITIVE THINKING PATTERNS

Young Ulrich grew up as an introverted lone wolf. In one of his many interviews he admits having had a *"deep intimacy with nature,"* despite the fact of growing up in a fairly big city.

He explained that one of the activities he most enjoyed was riding his bike after class and leaving behind what he called *"the miserable world of school."* He would then ride beyond the outskirts of the city and rest in a solitary place all by himself, where he would admire *"the world of nature"* with a single repetitive thought running over and over through his head:

"This will always be here, this will always be here."

Ulrich admitted having his first suicidal thoughts in primary school. He acknowledged repeatedly hearing the same fatidic questions, over and over in his mind:

"How can I eliminate myself from this world?"

"How can I commit suicide?"

Repeating these suicidal thoughts over and over became a habit for young Ulrich - and later an addiction! But he had no choice. He simply couldn´t stop repeating the same thoughts over and over!

It took Ulrich decades of inner struggle and suffering to finally break this addiction -we´ll see how in the following pages. In sum, he survived all right, but unfortunately many kids his age have not been so lucky:

> *A US study revealed that suicide is the fourth largest cause of mortality among children between the ages of 10 and 14. And according to two Swiss surveys approximately 3% of the boys and 8% of the girls between the age of 11 and 15 admitted to having attempted to end their lives at least once – even at the age of 7!*

ULRICH´S INNER STRUGGLE

Apart from suicidal thoughts that often came and went, Ulrich admitted that by the time he was ten he had already worked out several possibilities of how to kill himself.

During the years that followed, his suicidal urges persisted and he also experienced periods of intense depression. Finally, at the age of thirteen he refused to go to school any longer. He said it was too hostile and that he couldn´t take it anymore! So, he did not receive any form of formal education all through his teens and not before becoming a grown adult, when he finally decided to continue studying and actually managed to obtain a university degree in London.

But even that didn't satisfy him! He continued experiencing constant depressions and didn't know how to stop the recurrent suicidal thinking pattern he had picked up as a child!

TURNING LEAD INTO GOLD

As the years passed, Ulrich invariably continued experiencing severe depressions and suicidal crises. But finally, at the age of twenty-nine, he suffered the historic depression destined to forever transform his life.

Two things are for sure:

Ulrich never would have believed that one day he would break his suicidal thinking pattern literally overnight, like he did. And he never even imagined that he was destined to become one of the world's top authorities in the study of repetitive thoughts, mental patterns, suicidal tendencies, observation of the mind, breaking the habit of negative thinking, experiencing inner stillness and enjoying the joy of living and inner peace, as well as rediscovering the basis of what he later defined as the ancient alchemic secret of the *"transmutation of base metal into gold, of suffering into consciousness!"*

And yes, in case you still haven't guessed it or have no idea what I am talking about, the worldwide-famous spiritual guide and bestselling author **Ulrich Leonard Tolle**, is better known by his pen name **Eckhart Tolle**. He stands among the selected Great Masters consulted in this brief guidebook for beginners, which is humbly designed to help you begin to positively transform your life **starting today**!

Let us rejoice and contemplate eternity!

Namaste!

STEP 1

THE VALUE OF ADVERSITY

"Due to the ignorance of the real nature of one's own being, which is happiness itself, people struggle in the vast ocean of material existence, forsaking the right path that leads to happiness..."

Ramana Maharshi

153

A. J.   P A R R

THE FIRST STEP TO STOP NEGATIVE THINKING consists in accepting that adversity is part of the natural *"ups and downs"* of life and that it actually hides *"priceless lessons"* that can boost our spiritual progress and inner growth. Unfortunately, most people do not understand this and are swept away by the fierce waters of their own negativity.

In *"The Art of Happiness: A Handbook for Living"* (1998), the Dalai Lama states that *"the very purpose of our life is to seek (and attain) happiness."* He adds that as human beings *"we all desire happiness and not to suffer"* and that *"each individual has a right to pursue happiness and avoid suffering."*

But how can we truly attain happiness and end our suffering? Is this really possible?

To answer this question, as the Dalai Lama points out, above all we must understand that *"external circumstances are not what draw us into suffering"* and that *"suffering is caused and permitted by our own mind."*

Truth is, what we call "negative events" in our lives are not necessarily negative for they can actually impel our spiritual progress and transformation. We just saw Eckhart Tolle´s case. He never would have attained enlightenment had he not faced adversity in his childhood and youth

Eckhart admits that before turning thirty, back in his student days, he found himself continuously trapped in profound states of negative thinking that irremediably kept him *"deeply identified with thinking and the painful, heavy emotions accumulated within."* Back then, his mind was constantly flooded with pessimistic thoughts and his general negativity grew day by day. And despite the fact that he experienced a brief period of happiness and tranquility when he finished his studies and graduated, scarcely weeks later his *"unpleasant dream of thinking and painful emotions"* made their way back.

The return of this *"continuous anxiety interspersed with periods of suicidal depression"* soon triggered what Eckhart describes as a nightmarish state of depression and anxiety that literarily became unbearable. And that`s when, as he acknowledged, one night he heard *"the voice in his head"* repeatedly declaring once and again:

"I cannot live with myself any longer."

"I cannot live with myself any longer."

"I cannot live with myself any longer."

This was the reiterative thought that kept repeating itself in his mind, over and over, the night he decided to end his life without suspecting that this nightmarish state would soon change his fate drastically – not only affecting his own life, but millions around the globe!

WE CREATE OUR OWN HELL

What is "hell?" A subterranean realm filled with devils, flames and burning sinners or like most contemporary spiritual teachers claim, including Pope Francis, is it only a state of mind?

Four-hundred years ago, the English poet John Milton (1608-1674) tackled this question after tragically losing his sight at the age of 44 – just when he was starting to gain literary fame! To make things worse, scarcely three months after going completely blind, his wife died and soon, their one-year-old son followed.

John Milton was left completely shattered!

Not only was darkness all he could see, but another type of darkness now fell upon him: the darkness of suffering and growing despair, comparable to Eckhart´s *"continuous anxiety interspersed with periods of suicidal depression!"*

For less critical reasons many people have opted to take their own lives!

Driven by a lifelong quest for higher understanding, John Milton resisted what many would agree to call *"real Hell on Earth."* But instead of giving up on life, he turned his tragedy into

157

a valuable source of lessons that led the way for the adoption of new *"patterns of thinking and behaving."* He thus learned to see his cup half-filled instead of half-empty, turning darkness into light.

Not only did Milton remarry and father more children, but he also hired a secretary, resumed his writing career and in fact dictated his literary masterpiece, *"Lost Paradise"* in spite of total blindness, literally *"making a Heaven out of Hell."*

In his own words, as Milton declared in his celebrated book:

> **"The mind is its own place and in itself**
> **can make a Heaven of Hell, a Hell of**
> **Heaven."**

Regarding his personal tragedy and how he learned to cope with his loss of sight, he made the following confession in *"Lost Paradise"*:

> **"To be blind is not miserable; not to be**
> **able to bear blindness, that is miserable."**

As these pages explain in detail, the true source of pessimism is that most people do not know they are constantly *"making a Hell out of Heaven"* by continuously filling their heads with endless negative thoughts.

Why?

Because most people are continuously thinking about a *"better future"* or *"better past"* that only exists in their heads and which they nevertheless consider *"better than present reality,"* thus always leaving the *"real world"* in last place.

By continuously resisting and complaining, we unceasingly and indisputably believe *"we are better and worth more than this"* and that *"we deserve a better life."*

In summary, by perpetually filling our minds with thoughts of a better *"future life"* we recurrently reject the present and perceive it as *"inferior," "unsatisfactory," "insufficient," "incomplete," "undesirable,"* and even *"unbearable."* And repeatedly doing this has become a negative and sometimes fatal habit we cannot break!

TURNING LEAD INTO GOLD

Alchemy has been historically known as the ancient and legendary art of turning lead into gold. In ancient times it was studied by most respected men of science and with the passing of the centuries became the mother of modern chemistry and pharmacology.

However, according to the Swiss psychoanalyst Carl Jung, the ancient art does not refer to real gold and metals, but to the transformation of the human soul by turning ignorance into knowledge, unconsciousness into consciousness…

And that´s the secret of Alchemy, as we shall see in the following pages, the inner art of transmuting lead into gold, darkness into light, suffering into joy and, as John Milton claimed, Hell into Heaven!

FIRST EXERCISE

STOPPING YOUR THOUGHTS

The enquiry "Who am I?" is the principal means to the removal of all misery and the attainment of the supreme bliss. ...

Ramana Maharshi

IN THE MILLENARY INDIAN EPIC POEM known as the
Bhagavad Gita, in which Lord Krishna and his dear disciple,
prince Arjuna, discuss the difficulties of controlling the mind
before the start of the legendary battle of *Kurukshetra*.

The ancient Hindu chronicle starts out when Arjuna tells
Krishna he is full of doubts and cannot control his thoughts:

> *"Restless indeed is the mind!"* **Arjuna
> finally exclaims.** *"It is vehement, strong
> and unconquerable. Controlling it seems to
> me as hard as trying to control the wind!"*

To this, Krishna replied with words of wisdom:

> *"You speak the truth, Arjuna. Without
> doubt, the mind is restless and very difficult
> to restrain. But I can assure you that the
> mind can be controlled by constant practice
> and non-attachment..."*

STOPPING YOUR THINKING MIND

The following exercise consists in voluntarily stopping your
thoughts at least for 20 seconds and to see if you can.

To practice it, just follow these steps:

STEP 1:

Sit or lie down in a comfortable and relaxing position - the position you are now in will do – and then close your eyes before taking a deep breath to clear your mind.

Inhale… exhale…

STEP 2:

Mentally tell yourself that you will now stop thinking for at least 20 seconds just to prove you can and are in control.

STEP 3:

Mentally start counting from 1 to 20 and do your best not to have new thoughts. See how far you can go without having a single thought.

STEP 4:

While you count, one or more "*involuntary thoughts*" are bound to appear in your mind. Each time a new thought arises, stop counting.

Go back to the start and start counting from one all over again. So be alert, maintain a high level of inner awareness and stop every time a new thought arises.

For example:

> *"One, two, three, four, where did I leave my keys? Ooops! One, two, three, four, five, I'm doing better! Oh, no! One, two, three, four, five, six, seven, I'm hungry! For Christ's sake! One, two, three, etc."*

STEP 5:

If you can't do it the first time, repeat the process for at least three to five times. But don't worry, because if you fail to stop your thoughts, like most people, it does not mean you failed the exercise.

On the contrary, it means you succeeded, for this is what this practice is intended to prove (perhaps for the first time in your life) that you are not in complete control of your thoughts and that these can actually arise without your conscious awareness and control, as we will expand in the following lessons and exercises.

STEP 2

WE ARE WHAT WE THINK

"He who is enveloped by this veiling power (maya or illusion), wise or learned though he may be, clever, expert in the meaning of the scriptures, capable of wonderful achievements, will not be able to grasp the Truth..."

Ramana Maharshi

165

THE SECOND STEP OF STOPPING YOUR NEGATIVE THINKING consists in understanding that *"we are what we think"* and that we create our entire psychological reality based on a mental picture that only exists in our head!

To understand this, we must first consider that one thing is *"the real world"* and another completely different is *"the idea we have of the real world."*

The *"real world"* is the one and only reality or universal truth, while the second is nothing but a mental picture or *"illusory world"* that only exists in our heads!

Despite the fact that for centuries popular saying from all over the world have repeated more or less literally that *"every head is a world"* and that *"it all depends on the color of the glass you're looking through,"* most people have never stopped to think about the "real" implications of this.

It means that you and I, as well as everyone else on this planet, have a double-perception of reality: one real and the other only a psychological illusion we blindly take for real! And this illusion is precisely the radical source of human suffering and all our negative thoughts and behaviors, including our self-inflicted feelings of sadness, loneliness, hatred, regret, dissatisfaction, greed, anger, envy, fear, remorse, impatience and evilness.

167

Instead of experiencing reality as it truly is, every one of us has created an illusory world in his or her own mind, a *"fictitious representation of the world"* that only exists in our own head, as explained in the following pages, a creation of our own minds molded by our thoughts, ideals, beliefs, values, judgments and fears, among others.

Truth is, for thousands of years the Hindus have spoken of this *"illusory world"* created by our own mind and traditionally known as the "veil" or "dream of maya."

This state of illusion makes us perceive reality not *"as it truly is"* but as *"we think it is,"* according to our own personal and particular interpretations. For example, I may think buying a new car will make me a happy person, but my next-door neighbor may not be interested in getting a new car and perhaps actually believes he'll only be happy if he wins a political election or divorces his wife.

In the same fashion, every one of us has created a personal interpretation of our reality and what we think we need, creating a definite gap between *"the way we perceive things"* and *"the way things truly are."*

THE WORLD OF DELUSION

Most people spend their lives chasing success, fame, riches, power, pleasure, honor, social acceptance, excitement, respect and love, among other illusory dreams, hoping that these will one day grant them everlasting happiness and make their world a better place.

However, as the Hindu Sage Ramana Maharshi stated, these are vain pursuits for "*the world should be considered like a dream.*"

But why? Simply because each one of us, instead of experiencing reality as it truly is, have created an illusory world, a "*fictitious representation of the world*" that only exists within our own mind.

This "*fictitious representation of the world,*" as we shall see in the following pages, is the creation of our own minds and is molded by our thoughts, ideals, beliefs, values, judgments and fears, among others.

Truth is, for thousands of years the Hindus have spoken of this "*illusory world*" created by our own mind and traditionally known as the "veil" or "dream of maya."

As Ramana Maharshi explained:

"*Maya is that which makes us regard as non-existent the Self, the Reality, which is always and everywhere present, all-pervasive and self-luminous…*"

This state of illusion makes us perceive reality not "*as it truly is,*" but as "*we think it is,*" according to our own personal and particular interpretations. For example, I may think buying a new car will make me a happy person, but my next-door neighbor may not be interested in getting a new car and perhaps actually believes he´ll only be happy if he gets a new job or divorces his wife.

In the same fashion, every one of us has created a personal interpretation of our own reality and what we think we need, creating a definite gap between *"the way we think things are or should be"* and *"the way things truly are."*

Unfortunately, this mental perception of the world produces a *"distorted view of reality,"* generated and sustained by our own thoughts, especially by all the negative thoughts we constantly repeat, according to the following psychological principle:

> **"The more we repeat a specific thought about the world or ourselves, the more it affects our perception of the world and our self-image."**

Positive repetitive thoughts generate positive emotions when we think about them. But in the case of negative repetitive thoughts, these produce anxiety, depression, dissatisfaction, rage, chronic stress, as well as physical and mental disorders.

WE ARE WHAT WE THINK

According to the ancient legend, around 2,500 years ago the Buddha was the first to publicly proclaim that:

"We are what we think. All that we are arises with our thoughts and with our thoughts we make... "

Regarding this, the *Dvedhavitakka Sutta* gives us the following explanation:

"Whatever a monk pursues by thinking and considering, disposes his awareness.

"If a monk pursues thinking filled with sensuality, leaving behind thinking filled with renunciation, his mind will be bent by that thinking filled with sensuality.

"If a monk continuously pursues thinking filled with ill will, leaving behind thinking filled with non-ill will, his mind will be bent by that thinking filled with ill will.

"If a monk continuously pursues thinking filled with harmfulness, leaving behind thinking filled with harmlessness,

171

his mind will be bent by that thinking filled with harmfulness."

MADE BY THOUGHTS

Over two thousand years ago the celebrated Greek philosopher Epictetus (55-135 AD) stated:

"People are not disturbed by things, but by the view they take of them."

Similarly, the Roman leader Marcus Antonius (83-30 BC) conveyed this fact in his own words:

"Consider how much more you often suffer from your anger and grief, than from those very things for which you are angry and grieved."

In his own words, the Roman emperor and philosopher Marcus Aurelius Antoninus (121-180 AD) in his celebrated "*Meditations*" sustained:

"Our life is what our thoughts make it... If you are distressed by something external, the pain is not due to the thing itself but to your own opinion about it and thus you have the power to revoke it at

any moment... All we hear is just an opinion, not a fact. All we see is a perspective, not real truth."

Regarding this truth, the nineteenth-century American psychologist and philosopher William James (1842-1910) noted that *"man can alter his life by altering his thinking,"* adding that:

"Whilst part of what we perceive comes through our senses from the objects around us, another part (perhaps the larger) comes always from our own head."

Last but not least, the same truth was expressed by the British philosopher James Allen (1864-1912) in his bestselling book *"As Man Thinketh,"* in which he claimed that we are *"made and unmade"* by our own thoughts:

"Man is made or unmade by himself; in the armory of thought he forges the weapons by which he destroys himself; he also fashions the tools with which he builds for himself heavenly mansions of joy and strength and peace."

SECOND EXERCISE

WATCHING YOUR THOUGHTS

"You have probably come across 'mad' people in the street incessantly talking or muttering to themselves. Well, that's not much different from what you and all other 'normal' people do, except that you don't do it out loud. The voice comments, speculates, judges, compares, complains, likes, dislikes, and so on."

Eckhart Tolle

THE FOLLOWING BEGINNING EXERCISE will allow you to observe our thoughts as they arise and begin to experience your first *"gaps of inner stillness,"* as Eckhart Tolle explains:

> *"Start listening to the voice in your head as often as you can. This is what I mean by 'watching the thinker,' which is another way of saying: 'Listen to the voice in your head, be there as the witnessing presence.'"*

According to the nineteenth century Hindu monk Swami Vivekananda (1863-1902), unless we learn to tame our mind it will continuously jump around like a *"wild monkey,"*, forever swinging from branch to branch and jumping from thought to thought:

> *"How hard it is to control the mind! It has been well compared with the maddened monkey."*

Vivekananda recommended silently observing the mind and being aware of it *"bubbling up all the time"*:

> *"It is like that monkey jumping about. Let the monkey jump as much as he can; you simply wait and watch."*

WATCHING YOUR THOUGHTS

To do this exercise, just follow these steps:

FIRST:

Sit or lie down in a comfortable and relaxing position. The position you are now in while reading this book will do.

SECOND:

Close your eyes. Although you can also do this exercise with your eyes open, I recommend doing it with your eyes closed this first time to avoid unwanted distractions and increase your inner concentration.

Now say to yourself:

> ***"'I wonder what my next thought is going to be.' Then become very alert and wait for the next thought. Be like a cat watching a mouse hole. What thought is going to come out of the mouse hole? Try it now."***

THIRD:

Soon a new thought will appear in your head, for example: "*I'm thirsty*" or "*I'm having a thought.*"

FOURTH:

Whatever you do, first recognize that you are having a thought and then observe it without judging it or starting an inner conversation before letting it go and focusing your attention back to your inner state of alertness and silently wait for your next thought.

"Be like a cat watching a mouse hole."

FIFTH:

Repeat the process several times for one or two minutes, avoiding engaging in *"inner chat"* at all cost. Practicing this exercise, as we shall see in the following pages, will be most useful whenever you choose to make your repetitive negative thoughts lose their power over you, as *The Power of Now* indicates:

> *"As you listen to the thought, you feel a conscious presence - your deeper self - behind or underneath the thought, as it were. The thought then loses its power over you and quickly subsides, because you are no longer energizing the mind through identification with it."*

STEP 3

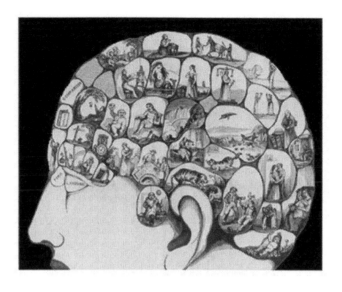

THE VOICE OF THE UNCONSCIOUS

"Maya is that which makes us regard as non-existent the Self, the Reality, which is always and everywhere present, all-pervasive and self-luminous..."

Ramana Maharshi

179

THE THIRD STEP OF STOPPING YOUR NEGATIVE THINKING consists in recognizing that all our thoughts are only words, symbols and mental pictures comparable to the words, symbols and pictures or personal computer.

Human thinking, as we all know, is fundamentally based on "words," which also constitute the basis of oral speech and written communication. However, words are only symbols.

But most people forget this.

The word "moon" for example, is used to represent the real moon. But it is not the actual moon. In fact, someone who has never seen the moon, or its picture cannot "imagine" the real moon unless he actually sees it. In any other case, his mental representation of the moon will necessarily be inaccurate, false.

Likewise, when we speak of "Truth" or "Illusion" there is no way you can truly understand their meaning unless you actually experience these.

It is said that the Buddha warned his followers not to try to rationally understand his teachings or to stick to his words, but to try to see beyond instead:

"My teaching is like a finger pointing to the moon. Do not mistake the finger for the moon."

As this simile states, "transcendental truth" cannot be expressed with words. Anything you believe or say about it is only "a finger pointing to the moon."

And since all words are merely "fingers pointing to the moon," we must be careful about what they mean.

Don´t be a fool, the Buddha states, the description of reality is not reality… The finger is not the point…: the point is the moon!

Therefore, don´t fall into the senseless trap of believing that your personal interpretation of reality and Truth is the absolutely reliable.

To understand the worthlessness of using words or reasoning when trying to communicate a direct experience try answering the following question:

Can you describe the flavor of chocolate to someone who has never tasted it?

It seems rather hard, doesn´t it?

Honestly, I find it totally impossible. No matter which words you use, your description will always be inaccurate and can never transmit what you are really trying to express: the flavor of chocolate to someone who has never tasted it.

In sum, the only way to understand what the flavor of chocolate is all about is by experiencing it, that is, by tasting it (direct experience).

Like the celebrated martial arts master and movie star Bruce Lee once said, paraphrasing the Budhha:

"Be like a finger pointing at the moon, but do not focus on the finger or you will miss all the heavenly glory."

THE PARABLE OF THE ARROW

According to Buddha, spiritual understanding can only be attained through direct experience and not through reasoning. In fact, trying to understand his teachings intellectually is actually an obstacle when trying to free yourself from the chains of illusion.

Similarly, freeing ourselves from the chains of illusion and attaining liberation cannot be described with words. It can only be understood by direct experience.

And that's what this book is all about: Finding inner peace, everlasting happiness and self-knowledge is not a matter of using words and symbols, but a matter of direct experience, as the following pages evidence.

OUR ENDLESS MENTAL CHATTER

Words are the essence of our endless mental chatter. This is why the Indian philosopher Jiddu Krisnamurti (1895-1986) usually referred to the thinking mind as the *"chattering mind,"* stating that this chatter is a constant process, an endless operation, and that *"every moment it is murmuring."*

In his 1954 best-seller *"The First and Last Freedom"* he stated:

> *"As I watch the brain, I see that the chattering happens only in the brain, it is a brain activity; a current flows up and down, but it is chaotic, meaningless and purposeless. The brain wears itself out by its own activity. One can see that it is tiring to the brain, but it does not stop... The mind chatters all the time and the energy devoted to that purpose fills a major part of our life.*
>
> *"The mind apparently needs to be occupied with something... The mind is occupied with something and if it is not occupied, it feels vacant, it feels empty and therefore it resorts to chattering..."*

THE VOICE IN THE HEAD

The source of our mental chatter is what Eckhart Tolle calls *"the voice in the head,"* which is seemingly produced in the hidden depths of our mind and hurled into the conscious levels without our voluntary control. Although this voice continuously comments, complains, guesses, judges, compares, approves and disapproves seemingly on its own, each thought is only the end result of a continuous and strictly automatic process based on the impulsive repetition of what he calls *"unconscious mental-emotional reactive patterns."*

Truth is, our repetitive negative thoughts are only *"reflexive reactions"* based on unconscious patterns of behavior conditioned by repetition, such as the act of continuously reviving a recent or distant undesirable past and thus causing self-inflicted suffering, sadness, regret, remorse, hatred or guilt or, on the other hand, the act of continuously imagining a possible negative situation in the future, often expecting things to go wrong and fearing a negative outcome thus causing self-inflicted pain, tension, worry, anxiety, fear, rage, stress and unhappiness, among other reflexive responses.

THE ROLE OF THE UNCONSCIOUS

The Father of Psychoanalysis, the Viennese neurologist Sigmund Freud based his revolutionary psychological theory on the fact that the human mind operates in two basic levels or layers: One is superficial, known as the "conscious," while the other lies hidden in the deepest layers of our minds, known as the "unconscious."

This dual nature of the mind is commonly explained by the *"iceberg metaphor,"* which states that the conscious is only the tip of the iceberg and that the enormous and unseen unconscious perennially hide beneath the surface.

185

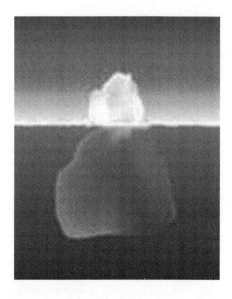

Just like a floating iceberg –or ice-cube for that matter–it mostly sinks down in the water with only a small part surfacing, which represents our conscious, which only constitutes a small part of our whole mind.

Freud was the first to announce that the workings of our thinking mind mostly take place in the deep and hidden layers of the unconscious – totally without our conscious awareness! He was also the first to compare the unconscious with a vast "storage-room" ("memory unit") where we keep all the information we have gathered and processed ever since we were born ("data"), including unconscious repetitive reactions based inner impulses.

According to him, our unconscious actually runs and controls our thinking mind and based on this he defined analytical therapy as the way of inducing mental sanity by *"turning unconscious processes into conscious awareness."*

THE MASTER OF YOUR MIND

In his *"Introduction to Psychoanalysis,"* Freud concludes what most people do not accept that the 'I' is not a *"master in its own home"* and that in reality we are governed by *"all that goes on unconsciously."*

"In the course of time humanity has had to withstand two great indignations against its naive self-love from the hands of science.

"The first took place when humans first discovered that our planet is not the center of this universe, but only a minute speck in a world-system hardly imaginable in its enormousness. We associate this with Copernicus, though Alexandrian scientists had already taught more or less the same.

"The second took place when biological research robbed man of his alleged superiority and special creation,

187

proving his descent from the animal kingdom and everlasting animal nature. This new vision, presented by Charles Darwin, Wallace and their predecessors, was not accepted without the most aggressive antagonism of their contemporaries.

"Nevertheless, the third and most irritating offence is presently being thrown against the human mania of greatness by psychological research, which is set to prove to the 'I' that it is not even master in its own home, but dependent on the scantiest information concerning all that goes on unconsciously in its psychic life."

"We psychoanalysts are not the first nor the only ones to announce the admonition to look within ourselves. It seems that we are destined to insistently prove this most insistently and confirm it by means of empirical data which to all individuals are of importance..."

OUR UNCONSCIOUS ASSUMPTIONS

According to Eckhart Tolle, the thinking mind is continuously processing thoughts and emotions in its deepest layers, generating all sorts of negative thoughts and reactive behaviors that continuously disturb us, based on by what he calls our *"unconscious assumptions"*:

> ***"'People cannot be trusted' would be an example of an unconscious assumption in a person whose primordial relationships, that is to say, parents or siblings, were not supportive and did not inspire trust."***

Psychologists have long found that the constant repetition of specific thoughts can actually "program" our minds–both positively and negatively–and that in fact these can *"distort our perception of reality,"* thus modifying our self-image and general state of wellbeing.

The influence of these repetitive thoughts was first studied by the American psychologist Albert Ellis, the second most influential psychologist of all times according to the American Psychological Association (APA), who in the mid-1950s based his Rational Emotive Behavior Therapy (REBT) on the premise that *"we largely feel according to the way we think."*

According to Ellis, people are influenced not by negative events but by their *"catastrophic"* repetitive thoughts and beliefs about these events. And these are always based on what he called *"irrational assumptions about what we must be and do."*

Among others, Eckhart mentions the following common *"unconscious assumptions"* in *The Power of Now*:

'Nobody respects or appreciates me'

'I need to struggle for survival

'I never have enough money'

'Life always lets me down'

'I don't deserve abundance'.

'I don't deserve love'

According to him, repeating these assumptions constantly transform or distort our personal reality without our awareness:

> **"Unconscious assumptions create emotions in the body which in turn generate mind activity and/or instant reactions. This way they create your personal reality...**

"The ego is not only the unobserved mind, 'the voice in the head' which pretends to be you, but also the unobserved emotions that are the body's reaction to what the voice in the head is saying. We have already seen what kind of thinking the egoic voice engages in most of the time and the dysfunction inherent in the structure of its thought processes, regardless of content.

"Dysfunctional thinking is what the body reacts to with negative emotion: The voice in the head tells a story that the body believes in and reacts to. Those reactions are the emotions. The emotions, in turn, feed energy back to the thoughts that created the emotion in the first place.

"Such is the vicious circle between our unexamined thoughts and emotions, thus giving rise to emotional thinking and emotional story-making. The emotional component of ego differs from person to person. In some egos, it is greater than in others..."

191

THIRD EXERCISE

BREATH MEDITATION

"Meditation is never the control of the body. There is no actual division between the organism and the mind. The brain, the nervous system and the thing we call the mind are one, indivisible. It is the natural act of meditation that brings about the harmonious movement of the whole. To divide the body from the mind and to control the body with intellectual decisions is to bring about contradiction, from which arise various forms of struggle, conflict and resistance..."

Krishnamurti

193

BREATH MEDITATION IS A HELPFUL PRACTICE based on becoming aware of our breath as it moves in and out of our body. Eckhart Tolle sustains in *A New Earth* that a single deep breath taken consciously, can slow down your thoughts and end your "inner chatter":

> *"One conscious breath is enough to make some space where before there was the uninterrupted succession of one thought after another. One conscious breath (two or three would be even better), taken many times a day, is an excellent way of bringing space into your life.*

BASIC STEPS OF THIS PRACTICE

Although the practice of breathing meditation or breath awareness has many different variations, all of them are based on consciously following *"the flow of your breath"*:

FIRST:

You can do this simple practice in any position you like: sitting, laying down, standing or in any position adopt while doing you regular daily routines, such as driving, walking, riding a vehicle or elevator, waiting on line or for an appointment, rushing up and down the steps at home or work, riding a bicycle, jogging, listening to music, washing your hands, bathing or simply while placidly resting in a park or beach.

SECOND:

Consciously take a few deep breaths concentrating on each time you inhale and exhale, following Eckhart′s basic guidelines:

"Don′t try judge or control your breath – realize that breathing isn't something you do but something you witness or observe. Breathing is autonomous and effortless. Your unconscious inner intelligence is in charge of it. Be the silent Witness, breathe and observe!"

"Even if you meditate on your breath for 2 hours or more - which some people do – a single breath is all you ever need to be aware of, indeed ever can be aware of. The rest is only memory or anticipation, that is to say, only thought."

THIRD:

Continue focused on each breath and whenever a new thought arises, simply be aware of it without getting "hooked" and let it go before turning your attention back to the physical sensation of *"your abdomen expanding and contracting slightly with each inhalation and exhalation."*

FOURTH:

Keep your attention focused on breathing consciously and repeat the process each time a new thought arises, until your flow of thoughts gradually slow down and you start to experience the silent gaps of inner stillness between thoughts (or between breaths), as detailed in *The Power of Now,* without ceasing to consciously:

> **"Feel yourself breathing into the lower abdomen and observe how it slightly expands and contracts with each in and out breath..."**

5: A more "visual" practice recommended by Eckhart consists in closing your eyes and consciously breathing while picturing yourself surrounded by a bright light or immersed in a luminous sea of consciousness before imagining yourself breathing or sinking in that light and starting to glow with intense brightness, as *The Power of Now* also instructs:

> **"Then gradually focus more on the feeling. Don't get attached to visual images. You are now in your body. You have accessed the power of Now."**

STEP 4

REPETITIVE NEGATIVE THINKING

"The brain wears itself out by its own activity. One can see that it is tiring to the brain, but it does not stop... The mind chatters all the time and the energy devoted to that purpose fills a major part of our life."

Krishnamurti

THE INFLUENCE OF OUR REPETITIVE NEGATIVE THOUGHTS and how they actually alter or distort our perception of the world and of ourselves was first studied in the 1960s by the American psychiatrist and University of Pennsylvania professor Aaron T. Beck, better known as the Father of Cognitive Therapy.

Beck gave these altered perceptions the name of "*cognitive distortions*" and concluded they are exclusively sustained by the regular repetition of common negative thoughts such as:

"I feel so lonely!"

"I will never be happy".

"I need to be accepted."

"People always take advantage of me."

"I always have bad luck."

"I feel so depressed!"

"I am so angry"

"I cannot do anything right!"

"I will never succeed!"

"I will never be happy!"

"Nobody cares about me!"

"No one will ever love me!"

"No one understands me!

"Nobody can be trusted."

"I'm truly unattractive or ugly."

"I'm a loser!"

"He or she does not like or accept me."

"I'm so stupid!"

"I hate myself!"

"I can't stand it!"

THE TWO SIDES OF THE COIN

To understand how repetitive thinking affect us let's imagine the following example: Suppose an important bank hires a couple of young executives, both fresh out of college: the twin brothers Bill and Joe Smith.

The twins not only look exactly alike but also have the same physical and mental conditions and potentials. Their only big difference, however, lies in the nature of their thoughts:

Let´s start with Bill. Unlike his brother he is always repeating to himself positive or optimistic thoughts like:

"I´m so glad I´m alive"

"I´m so happy"

"I have and important purpose in live"

"No pain no gain"

"People always like me"

"Each time I fail I am one step closer to success"

On the other hand, although both grew up with the same parents, his brother Joe somehow ended up being a pessimist and is always repeating negative thoughts to himself like:

"I hate my life"

"I can´t do it"

"I´ll always have bad luck"

"Nobody will ever love me"

"I'll never be happy"

And so, while Bill always sees a half-full glass, Joe always sees it half-empty.

Fact is, Bill sees a world of opportunities and success, whereas Joe only sees a world of failure and sadness.

Which of the two do you think is more likely to succeed in life? And who seems more likely to fail and suffer?

TWO DIFFERENT WORLDS

As we have seen, Bill and Joe actually live in two different worlds despite their similar conditions and have very different perceptions of themselves.

Due to Joe´s negative thoughts, he perceives himself as a potential failure, unable to reach success, while Bill perceives himself as a successful man willing to overcome problems and work his way to success.

Both brothers have fabricated a mental image of themselves, each based on personal ideas and imagination: one is optimistic and the other pessimistic. But the fact that both these images were imaginary does not stop them from producing "real" consequences in their psyches.

Joe is possessed by his own pessimism, and his repetitive negative thoughts only sink him deeper and deeper in his dream of illusion. He represents the state of mind maintained by most people in the world, who unconsciously repeat negative thoughts without analyzing their origin or knowing how these can disturb them.

Joe's dream of himself undoubtedly affects him deeply, creating self-inflicted suffering, insecurity, despair, rage, fear, and depression, among other consequences. He obviously perceives that *something is always missing in life* and feels *incomplete.* Because of this he always tries to find happiness in exterior objects, pleasures or people, believing that one day he will satisfy his most-esteemed desires and experience everlasting happiness and peace of mind.

What's Joe's biggest mistake?

Not realizing that he is only imagining things!

In reality, Joe has the same conditions and chances of succeeding as his brother. In fact, he has all he needs to experience true happiness here and now. But ignoring this truth constitutes his main problem.

Unfortunately, most of us are just like Joe.

Influenced by our repetitive negative thoughts, we too have created a false perception of the world and of ourselves. And the more we think about and believe in these false perceptions, the more they will end up affecting us with negative emotions, as Eckhart explains:

"Almost every human body is under a great deal of strain and stress, not because it is threatened by some external factor but from within the mind."

FOURTH EXERCISE

FEELING THE INNER BODY

"What I call the "inner body" isn't really the body anymore but life energy, the bridge between form and formlessness. Make it a habit to feel the inner body as often as you can."

Eckhart Tolle

205

ECKHART TOLLE RECOMMENDS stopping our endless flow of thoughts by experiencing what he calls our *"inner body."* According to him, this is a fast and sure way of connecting with the Now by slowing down our thoughts and our *"mind chatter."* And learning to do this at will is precisely what this exercise is all about!

According to Eckhart, to experience your inner body you must keep in mind a couple of basic principles:

*The body is a vehicle for experiencing Presence.

*You cannot experience Presence through your thoughts.

To practice this exercise, follow these steps, as Eckhart indicates:

FIRST:

Close your eyes. Now concentrate on *"feeling"* your right hand without moving it.

Where is it? How can you know if it's there? Instead of moving it, concentrate on *"feeling"* its aliveness. Do it now!

If you do this for several seconds, you will start to experience a slight *"inner tingling"* or *"inner warmth"* in your hand. Eckhart calls it *"your inner sense of aliveness," "inner presence,"* or *"being-ness."*

Concentrate. Feel it. Experience it.

SECOND:

As you continue feeling this inner *"tingling"* or *"warmth"* in your hand, be observant and wait for your next thought.

"Be like a cat watching a mouse hole."

THIRD:

Each time a new thought arises, observe it, avoid judging or starting an inner conversation. Then simply let it go and bring back your attention to the feeling of inner aliveness within your hand.

FOURTH:

Although Eckhart recommends focusing on the hands, it really doesn't matter which part of your body you focus on. What's important is that you take your focus away from your thoughts and concentrate on something physical.

Now, also direct your attention to your other hand and silently concentrate on feeling the aliveness within.

Can you feel it?

Gradually include the rest of your body, beginning with your arms and slowly including your feet, your legs, your trunk and your head.

FIFTH:

Silently concentrate on the subtle energy field pervading your entire body. Feel it in all parts of your body simultaneously, as a single field of energy.

Don't think about it. Just feel it!

This is what Eckhart calls *"inner-body awareness."*. According to him, and as I have experienced countless times, the more you practice this form of meditation, the clearer and stronger your experience will get:

> *"You may get an image of your body becoming luminous. Although such an image can help you temporarily, pay more attention to the feeling than to any image that may arise. An image, no matter how beautiful or powerful, is already defined in form, so there is less scope for penetrating more deeply."*

SIXTH:

Repeat this practice as often as you can for several days (at least a minute each time). You can do this at work or home, while driving, walking, jogging, riding the elevator, waiting on line or simply relaxing, among others.

The more you practice the more you will get in touch with what Eckhart calls your *"inner sense of aliveness,"* allowing you to temporarily leave all your thoughts and worries behind and start to gradually intensify the joyful feeling of experiencing the *Now*!

STEP 5

TRAPPED IN PAST AND FUTURE

"One does not become a king by merely saying, 'I am a king,' without destroying one's enemies and obtaining the reality of power. Similarly, one does not obtain liberation... without destroying the duality caused by ignorance and directly experiencing the Self."

Ramana Maharshi

THE FOURTH STEP OF STOPPING YOUR NEGATIVE THINKING consists in learning to avoid getting *"stuck in time"* and thus escape from the traps of our past and future, which always causes us to sink into pessimism and distorts our view of reality.

Regarding the fact of being *"stuck in time"* and its negative consequences, over half a century ago the outstanding American writer Helen Keller (1880-1968), who went deaf and blind when she was only an infant and nevertheless reached world-wide fame as a prominent author and social activist, expressed:

> *"When one door of happiness closes, another opens; but often we look so long at the closed door that we do not see the one which has been opened for us..."*

THE HABIT OF EVADING REALITY

By thinking continuously in our past (as well as in our future) we constantly evade reality. And by doing this we automatically neglect the present moment and always end up rejecting and even despising it!

Like most contemporary humans, we first adopted the habit of evading reality through constantly thinking when we were small children and have repeated this same pattern each time we have felt unsatisfied with the present moment for some reason or another.

In countless cases we have "compensated" us in satisfaction by losing ourselves in our own thoughts, imagining better times or remembering a longed-for past. And this precisely makes us neglect and resist to "what is."

A person with predominantly negative thoughts, as Eckhart Tolle points out, reflects an unevolved mind, that is, a primitive state of consciousness characterized by ignorance.

Since ancient times this *"untrained state of awareness"* has been compared with being *"asleep," "blind," "dreaming," "unconscious," "ignorant,"* or *"in darkness.""*

Truth is we are all blind to certain degree. And as metaphorically described by John Milton, unless we awaken and accept "reality as it is" without resisting, we will always turn heaven into hell, as Eckhart Tolle suggests in *The Power of Now*:

> *"If you found yourself in paradise, it wouldn't be long before your mind would say 'yes, but...'"*

THE DISEASE OF PSYCHOLOGICAL TIME

In 1968, Krishnamurti expressed the following during a series of talks he delivered in Puerto Rico:

> *"Psychological time only exists when there is comparison, when there is a distance to be covered between 'what is' and 'what should be', which is the desire to become somebody or nobody, all that involves psychological time and the distance to be covered."*

To avoid negative thoughts and feelings he gave the following recommendation:

> *"When you have some experience of joy, of pleasure or whatever it is, live it completely and do not demand that it should endure, because then you are caught in time."*

POSTPONING HAPPINESS

Most humans are always postponing their own happiness for they believe they do not deserve it and that they will only be happy sometime in the future. But only if they reach certain goal, become rich, buy a new car or home, get a juicy raise or a better job, get married or start a romantic relationship, win the lottery, or satisfy this or that other craving. As Carl Jung explains in the introduction of Heinrich Zimmer´s "*The Way to the Self*":

> *"Once he launches himself in pursuit of external things, man is never satisfied, as evidenced when dealing with our bare necessities. He is always in pursuit of more and more and, true to his own prejudices, he always looks for that more in external things.*

> *"He forgets completely that, in spite of all the external success, he remains the same inside, and thus complains about his poverty if he just owns a single car instead of two, like his neighbors. Undoubtedly, providing ourselves with everything that is necessary is a source of happiness that we should not underestimate.*

> *"But above all, and transcending it, the inner man cries out that no external good can satisfy us; and the less attention is paid to this voice, in the middle of the hunt for the "wonderful things" of this world, the more the inner man creates an*

inexplicable source of bad luck and incomprehensible sorrow, while living a life of living conditions we could expect to produce something very different.

CRAVING FOR TOMORROW

Continuously craving for a *"better future"* automatically degrades our perception of the real world and the Now. Comparing the present moment with better times always makes it seem inferior and less desirable. This is why Eckhart Tolle explains that the road to awakening lies beyond judgments and comparisons. It consists in concentrating on being Present and on connecting yourself to the endless and ever generous flow of *"what is"*:

"All cravings are the mind seeking salvation or fulfillment in external things and in the future as a substitute for the joy of Being."

MANAGING GOALS AND DESIRES

No matter what you expect to gain from these teachings, there is no need to give up your desires or stop working to fulfill them.

If the future and all we think about it is only an illusion, then what should we do? Does it mean we should completely stop thinking about tomorrow, avoid desiring things and forget all impending plans?

Not at all!

It only means, as we will see in the following pages, that above all you need to pursue your goals without overvaluation and overexcitement, recognizing the difference between clock time and psychological time and always keeping in mind that you do not depend on the future to experience the joy of Being here and now:

"If you set yourself a goal and work toward it, you are using clock time. You are aware of where you want to go, but you honor and give your fullest attention to the step that you are taking at this moment.

"If then you become excessively focused on the goal, perhaps because you seek happiness, fulfillment or a more complete sense of self, the Now is no longer honored. It becomes reduced to a mere stepping stone to the future without intrinsic value.

"Clock time then turns into "psychological time." Your life's journey no longer is an adventure, only an obsessive need to arrive, to attain, to 'make it.'

"You no longer see or smell the flowers by the wayside either. Nor are aware of the beauty and the miracle of life unfolding around you when you are present in the Now."

A. J.   P A R R

FIFTH EXERCISE

THE TIMELESS GAP

"If you no longer want to create pain for yourself and others, if you no longer want to add to the residue of past pain that still lives on in you, then don't create any more time, or at least no more than is necessary to deal with the practical aspects of your life..."

Eckhart Tolle

**TWO   OF   ECKHART   TOLLE'S   MAIN   BASIC
PRINCIPLES** are that *"time and mind are inseparable"* and that
*"remove time from the mind and it stops - unless you choose to use
it!"*

But how on earth can we actually remove time from the mind?

Is this even possible?

Yes, according to Eckhart, who claims that doing this is
relatively simple with some practice: All it takes is learning to
"read between the lines" and experience the *"silent gap"* between
thoughts. To understand and personally experience this, just follow
these steps:

FIRST:

Observe your thoughts as most as you can during your daily
routine. Identify your most frequent *"repetitive negative thoughts"*
and write them down. This list will help you detect the thoughts
you need to avoid.

Is there a predominant and repetitive thought present in your
daily thinking? What is it? Is it directly or indirectly related with
your present unhappiness?

SECOND:

Each time you find yourself repeating a same negative thought or thoughts over and over in your mind or engaged in *"negative mental chatter,"* remember it is you *"voice in the head"* repeating the same *"negative thinking pattern"* you have repeated for years (probably since you were a kid).

Realize it is not you who is doing the actual thinking and that your repetitive inner thoughts are only *"conditioned responses"* or *"reflexive reactions"* produced by your ego or *"thinking mind."*

THIRD:

Next, immediately recognize that you are the owner of your mind and therefore always have the right to join or not in a mental conversation with your *"voice in the head."* You both have and deserve that right – yours is the right to choose!

FOURTH:

Momentarily stop judging your own thoughts and avoid talking back or starting all inner dialogue. Now that you know better, don't fall into the trap and consciously give it a no and refuse to participate.

To help you do this just follow the next step:

FIFTH:

As you continue observing your thoughts, now concentrate on the "silent gap between one and the next. These gaps of complete silence are *"glimpses of inner stillness"* and within them there is no thinking. Hence, no future nor past! Just a non-verbal consciousness of "Being" or "Presence," as Eckhart calls it.

The world's main spiritual teachings mention the supreme importance of these silent gaps of inner stillness. They are also known as the "sound" or "voice" of *silence."* Among these teachings, Eckhart includes those of Krishna, Buddha, Jesus, Rumi, Lao-Tze, Meister Eckhart, Ramana Maharshi, Krishnamurti, and *A Course In Miracles.*

SIXTH:

Concentrate on the silent gap for a few seconds. Simply concentrate on the total silence between one thought and the next. Be cautious for this silence may only last a brief instant, as mentioned in *Stillness Speaks*:

> *"Pay attention to the gap, the gap between two thoughts, the brief, silent space between words in a conversation, between the notes of a piano or flute, or the gap between the in-breath and the out-breath. When you pay attention to*

those gaps, awareness of 'something' becomes just awareness. The formless dimension of pure consciousness arises from within you and replaces identification with form."

What does it feel like? You have a thought here, a thought there, and between each there's a little space, a blank or silent gap. Initially the experience may only last a second or even brief microseconds, so please pay close attention.

How long should the gaps ideally be? Don´t worry about it! As Eckhart explains in *A New Earth:*

"You need not be concerned with the duration of those gaps. A few seconds is good enough. These will gradually lengthen themselves without effort on your behalf. More important than their length is bringing them in frequently so that your daily activities and stream of thinking become interspersed with space."

Eckhart describer that initially these silent gaps will be brief, only a few seconds perhaps. Nevertheless, with practice they will gradually become longer:

SEVENTH:

Repeat this exercise several times a day, preferably combining it with breath or inner body meditation, until managing to gradually experience longer gaps.

Each time a new thought arises, repeat the same process: Don´t judge it. Don´t engage in *"mental chatter."* Just observe it, release it and then concentrate once more on experiencing the *"timeless gap between thoughts."*

By doing this, you will actually slow down and even stop your usual stream of thoughts and cease comparing the present moment with an imaginary *"before or after."*

And thus, you will truly begin to free yourself from the trap of psychological time and the human compulsion of *"endless preoccupation with past and future and an unwillingness to honor and acknowledge the present moment and allow it to be"*:

> **"The compulsion arises because the past gives you an identity and the future holds the promise of salvation, of fulfillment in whatever form. Both are illusions."**

STEP 6

NEGATIVITY AND RESISTANCE

"While dreaming, all kinds of things may come to mind, but these are nothing more than appearances. Likewise, a magician may create a variety of illusory appearances, but they do not exist objectively..."

Dalai Lama

THE SIXTH STEP OF STOPPING NEGATIVE THINKING consists in learning to surrender without resistance to the endless flow "what if," as Eckhart Tolle describes in *The Power of Now*:

> *"Surrender is the simple but profound wisdom of yielding to rather than opposing the flow of life... The only place where you can experience the flow of life is the Now."*

What does Eckhart mean?

That we need to accept the present moment unconditionally ("Thy Will Be Done"); relinquishing all inner resistance to "*what is*":

THE NEED TO SURRENDER

To avoid negativity and experience inner joy you must first learn to surrender. However, this does not mean "*throwing the towel*" or "*giving up on life*" as Eckhart explains:

> *"Surrender is perfectly compatible with taking action, initiating change or achieving goals. But in the surrendered state a totally different energy, a different quality, flows into your doing."*

229

Surrender means recognizing the illusory nature of our thoughts and desires; it means accepting things as they truly are and not as we imagine them to be. It means yielding to unexpected changes in life rather than opposing and resisting to them.

It means unconditionally accepting the present moment and what is real "here and now."

It also means accepting reality as it is by ceasing to compare it with ideal future or past realities that only exist in your head.

So, give up waiting as tour "normal" state of mind.

Snap out of it and step out of the time into the present and "*just be and enjoy being,*" as Eckhart recommends:

> **"You might say, 'What a dreadful day,' without realizing that the cold, the wind, and the rain or whatever condition you react to are not dreadful. They 'are as they are'.**
>
> **What is dreadful is only your reaction and inner resistance to it, and the emotion created by this resistance."**

INNER TRANSFORMATION

Inner transformation can only take place here and now. You cannot postpone it without losing it. Regarding this transformation, the Indian philosopher and spiritual teacher Jiddu Krishnamurti (1895-1986) sustained in his celebrated book *"The First and Last Freedom"*:

> *"Transformation is in the future, can never be in the future. It can only be now, from moment to moment... When you see that something is false, that false thing drops away... As we are surrounded by so much that is false, perceiving the falseness from moment to moment is transformation.*

A. J.   P A R R

SIXTH EXERCISE

SURRENDERING TO THE NOW

"Let me summarize the process. Focus your attention on the feeling inside you... Don't think about it - don't let the feeling turn into thinking. Don't judge or analyze... Be aware not only of the emotional pain but also of 'the one who observes,' the silent watcher. This is the power of the Now, the power of your own conscious presence. Then see what happens."

Eckhart Tolle

ACCORDING TO ECKHART TOLLE, surrendering to the Now means consciously accepting the present moment *"as it is."* But not by passive resignation! It means ceasing to base your happiness on a *"cherished future"* or a *"cherised past"* and ending all resistance to the Now, as he briefly indicates:

> *"The basis for effective action is to come into an inner alignment with the 'is-ness' of this moment: This is how it is."*

This inner alignment has been known for centuries and received many names.

Jesus called it surrendering our will to God by accepting that *"Thy will be done on Earth as it is in Heaven."*

Meister Eckhart defined it as *"letting go of one self"* through the cessation of **self**-will and the gradual acquirement of what he called an *"empty spirit."*

Carl Jung called it *"the art of letting things happen"* and highlighted its importance for the healthy mind:

> *"The art of letting things happen, action through nonaction, letting go of oneself, as taught by Meister Eckhart, became for me the key opening the door to the way.*

"We must let things happen in our psyche. For us, it is actually an art of which scarce persons know anything. Consciousness is incessantly interfering."

Last but not least *A Course in Miracles,* which Eckhart practiced back in London during his beginning days as spiritual teacher and still recommends to those in need of higher understanding, calls this *"placing the future in the Hands of God"* (your inner Divinity or Ultimate Reality) and bases this transcendental experience on following these three steps:

FIRST:

Recognize that God holds your future as He holds your past and present:

"They are one to Him, and so they should be one to you. Yet in this world, the temporal progression still seems as real. And therefore, you are not asked to understand the lack of sequence really found in time."

SECOND:

Instead of trying to control your life leave everything in God´s Hands:

"You are only asked to let the future go and place it in God's Hands. And you'll see by experience that you have laid the past and present in His Hands as well, for the past will punish you no more, and future dread will now be meaningless.

"Release the future, for the past is gone. And what is present, freed from its bequest of grief and misery, of pain and loss, becomes the instant in which time escapes the bondage of illusions, where it runs its pitiless, inevitable course... Place, then, your future in the Hands of God...."

THIRD:

Repeat to yourself several times a day or as often as you can the following statement, especially each time you catch your *"voice in the head"* repeating a negative and undesired thought or if you find yourself irremediably lost in a continuous and pessimistic mental conversation or chatter:

"I place the future in the Hands of God"

TO EACH DAY ITS OWN TROUBLES

According to his celebrated *Sermon of the Mount*, Jesus metaphorically stressed the importance of freeing ourselves from the trap of time and ceasing to worry about the future by surrendering to "*what is*":

> *"So, this I say to you, do not worry about your life, what you will eat or what you will drink; nor about your body or what you will wear. Is not your life worth more than your food and your body more than your clothes?*

> *"Watch the birds of the skies, for they neither plant nor obtain nor gather in barns. And yet your heavenly Father feeds them. Are you not worth more than they? Which of you can add a single cubit to his height? So, why do you worry about clothing?*

> *"Contemplate the lilies of the field and how they grow: they neither work nor weave; and yet I say to you that even Solomon in all his glory never did dressed like one of these!"*

"Now if God so dresses the meadow of the field, which today grows and tomorrow burns in the furnace, will He not dress you better, O men of poor faith?

"Therefore, stop worrying and saying: 'What will we eat?' or 'What will we drink?' or 'What will we wear?' Gentiles seek these things. But your heavenly Father knows what you need. So first seek the kingdom of God and His righteousness, and all these things will be added to you.

"So, cease to worry about tomorrow, for tomorrow will worry about its own things. Enough for the day is its own trouble!"

STEP 7

EXPERIENCING THE JOY OF LIVING

"As soon as you honor the present moment, all unhappiness and struggle dissolve, and life begins to flow with joy and ease."

Eckhart Tolle

A. J. P A R R

THE SEVENTH STEP OF STOPPING NEGATIVE THINKING consists in learning to experience the Joy of Living.

As the XIV Dalai Lama admits, the biggest difference between common westerners and Tibetan lamas, as well as the biggest difference is that we constantly experience what the lamas call *"ceaseless streams of thoughts,"* just like they do, only that they *"choose not to listen"*:

> ***"Even the high Lamas of Tibet experience the ceaseless stream of thoughts running through our minds. The only difference is, we don't listen."***

Similarly, an ancient Chinese proverb has anonymously claimed for thousands of years:

> ***"You cannot prevent the birds of sorrow from flying over your head, but you can prevent them from building nests in your hair."***

This ancestral metaphor symbolizes that we cannot avoid having negative thoughts every now and then. However, we can learn to ignore them as soon as they appear in our minds by consciously avoiding in these cases to engage yourself in useless "inner chat" with the voice in your head - thus stopping the "*birds of sorrow*" from "*building nests in your hair.*"

THE CREATIVE USE OF MIND

Now that you have learned how to slow down your flow of thoughts and avoid the traps of repetitive negative thinking, you are free to use your mind creatively in your daily life, when solving problems, making a decision or overcoming obstacles, as Eckhart explains:

> *"If you need to use your mind for a specific purpose, use it in conjunction with your inner body. Only if you can be conscious without thought can you use your mind creatively, and the easiest way to enter that state is through your body.*
>
> *"Whenever an answer, a solution, or a creative idea is needed, stop thinking for a moment by focusing attention on your inner energy field. Become aware of the stillness.*

*"When you resume thinking, it
will be fresh and creative. In any
thought activity, make it a habit to
go back and forth every few
minutes or so between thinking
and an inner kind of listening, an
inner stillness.*

*"Don't just think with your
head, think with your whole
body."*

THE SECRET OF HAPPINESS

The problem with most people is that they believe themselves to
be dependent on what happens for their own happiness.

On the contrary, as announced around half a century ago by the
Indian enlightened spiritual teacher Jiddu Krishnamurti, you can
experience happiness here and now if you avoid caring about what
happens and simply accept the present moment *"as it is."*

This is one way of saying that above all we need to turn the
Now into our dear friend instead of our dark enemy, in alignment
with *"what is"*, as Eckhart details:

*"When we befriend the present moment
with acceptance and non-resistance, we will*

feel more peaceful and be less torn by what we like and don't like. To be happier, make friends with what is…

"Accept the present moment and find the perfection that is deeper than any form and untouched by time…

"The joy of Being, which is the only true happiness, cannot come to you through any form, possession, achievement, person, or event—through anything that happens.

"That joy cannot come to you—ever. It emanates from the formless dimension within you, from consciousness itself and thus is One With Who You Are."

SEVENTH EXERCISE

BEATING NEGATIVE THINKING

"For some, the awakening happens as they suddenly become aware of the kinds of thoughts they habitually think, especially persistent negative thoughts that they may have been identified with all of their lives. Suddenly there is an awareness that is aware of thought but is not part of it."

Eckhart Tolle

THE FOLLOWING STEPS condense the basic teachings presented in this book, designed to help you beat pessimism and adequately face negative obstacles and casualties with the *Power of Now*:

FIRST:

The next time you find yourself facing times of trouble and adversity, do not despair! Begin by avoiding all impulsive reactions and take a deep breath instead.

Become the Watcher of your thoughts as you breathe and avoid blindly following the negative impulses that may arise, which are always pre-determined by what Eckhart Tolle calls *"unconscious mental-emotional reactive patterns."*

A single deep breath will help you increase your alertness and interrupt your *"inner chat,"* as Eckhart advices:

> *"This can start with a very simple thing, such as taking one conscious breath... so that there is no mental commentary running at the same time..."*

SECOND:

Remember that *"you are what you think"* and that instead of perceiving *"reality as it is"* your thinking mind always interprets everything in terms of *"what you think it i.s.* Avoid reacting based on the *"illusory sense of how you should react"* and instead of blindly repeating your usual negative patterns, concentrate on following your breaths.

THIRD:

Keep breathing consciously and closely observing your *"voice in the head."* No matter what it says or how it reacts, avoid getting hooked on mental dialogues and watch out for any *"repetitive thinking pattern,s,* which Eckhart describes as *"those old audiotapes that have been playing in your head perhaps for many years."*

FOURTH:

As you continue breathing consciously, accept your present situation without getting stuck in it and realize that it is completely natural for things not to always necessarily turn out as expected. So, stop reacting immaturely and do your best to see the glass half-full instead of half-empty, as Eckhart suggests:

> **"It is true that my present life situation is the result of things that happened in the past, but it is still my present situation, and being**

stuck in it is what makes me unhappy."

FIFTH:

Avoid thinking about a better future or past and their countless *"what ifs"* by concentrating in the Now. Do not compare your present situation with an imagined reality, no matter what, for this always postpones your own happiness instead of allowing you to experience the joy of Being right here and now.

SIXTH:

Turn to the inner energy gently vibrating within your hand and sink in the Now without resistance, accepting that this always leads to a *"higher understanding of things"* compatible with acting, solving problems and accomplishing immediate goals.

SEVENTH:

Finally, feel your inner feeling of aliveness growing within you and filling your whole body with a *"subtle emanation of joy arising from deep within,"* as Eckhart notes:

> **"When these gaps occur, you feel a certain stillness and peace inside you. This is the beginning of your natural state of felt**

oneness with Being, which is usually obscured by the mind.

"With practice, the sense of stillness and peace will deepen. In fact, there is no end to its depth. You will also feel a subtle emanation of joy arising from deep within: the joy of Being."

Your inner aliveness is the gateway to the joy of Living. Feel it silently vibrating within you. Do you sense its aliveness? Can you feel the subtle joy?

Yes, it is time to give yourself permission to be happy here and now! You deserve it! It is your right!

Remain in the gap and focus on experiencing the joy of Being vibrating within you and flowing from your heart!

There is no longer a need to keep waiting to experience happiness. So, forget your self-imposed barriers and excuses! Start being happy here and now!

It is time to awaken!

Open your eyes and realize that, no matter what, everything is perfect! Better impossible, for nothing exists other than the Now!

Remain in the gap as long as you can and repeat this each day as many times as you decide and begin to experience your inner transformation with the Power of Now!

ABOUT THE AUTHOR

IN MY OWN WORDS

A. J. PARR is a journalist, comparative religion researcher and indie author with a lifelong interest and experience in meditation techniques:

I RECEIVED MY FIRST HINDU INITIATION when I was 17 years old (I am now 60), in the *Mission of the Divine Light*, founded back in the 70s by Guru Maharaj Ji (presently known as *Prem Rawat*). His basic teachings included four different meditation techniques to stop the mind and free us from Illusion.

I was almost 30 when I received my second Hindu initiation and meditation technique, this time from a disciple of Maharishi Mahesh Yogi (1918-2008), creator of Transcendental Meditation or TM. It must be said that Maharishi´s "*mantra meditation*" technique was practiced, among others, by the Beatles, Mia Farrow, Shirley MacLaine, Donovan, and Deepak Chopra, who worked side by side with Maharishi before starting his own career as a spiritual guide. That year, I also joined the Freemasonry and continued in its files until obtaining, several years later, the Sublime Degree of Master Mason

At the age of 37, I received my third Eastern initiation and meditation technique, this time from the Sant Mat tradition, also known as *"The Path of Saints,"* derived from Hinduism and Sikhism.

Finally, during the last decade, I have studied *"A Course in Miracles"* together with the teachings of Eckhart Tolle, Deepak Chopra, Dalai Lama, Ramana Maharshi and Krishnamurti, among others, experiencing the inner transformation and understanding that finally gave birth to *"The Secret of Now Series."*

Contact the author at: edicionesdelaparra@gmail.com

THE SECRET OF NOW SERIES

VOLUME 1

Living in "The Now" in Easy Steps

https://www.amazon.com/dp/B00J57TQZO

VOLUME 2

Buddhist Meditation For Beginners

https://www.amazon.com/dp/B00JE54A8K

VOLUME 3

Spiritual Hindu Tales to Calm Your Mind

https://www.amazon.com/dp/B00JJZLCBI

VOLUME 4

Christian Meditation in Easy Steps

https://www.amazon.com/dp/B00KLHUG7Y

VOLUME 5

Meditation in 7 Easy Steps

https://www.amazon.com/dp/B01L9DRF9U

VOLUME 6

Stop Negative Thinking in 7 Easy Steps

https://www.amazon.com/dp/B00MVLI6JI

THANKS IN ADVANCE!

Let us rejoice and contemplate eternity!

NAMASTE!

PUBLISHED BY:

GRAPEVINE BOOKS
EDICIONES DE LA PARRA

69485006R00156

Made in the USA
Middletown, DE
06 April 2018